EMPOWERING CHANGE:

A Guide to Cultivating Your Nonprofit Business

Dr. Beverly M. Griffor

Bandor Books

Ann Arbor, Michigan

www.bandorbooks.com

Library of Congress Control Number: 2025945538

ISBN 979-8-9997341-2-9 (paperback)
ISBN 979-8-9997341-3-6 (ebook)

First Edition

Printed in the United States of America

Cover art and design by Valentina Pino

Disclaimer:
This book is intended for informational purposes only. This is not legal advice. The author and publisher are not responsible for any actions taken based on the information contained herein. Readers should consult qualified professionals before implementing any practices described.

Published by Bandor Books
Ann Arbor, MI
www.bandorbooks.com

**BANDOR
BOOKS**

To my family, for your years of unwavering love, patience, and belief in my work.

To every changemaker who sees what could be, and works tirelessly to make it what is.

CONTENTS

PRELUDE

People of conviction and purpose often see the world as it could be. Starting a nonprofit business allows you to address social concerns, have a positive influence, and effect real change. Nonprofits are driven by a goal and aim to address unmet needs in areas such as education, healthcare, poverty reduction, and environmental conservation. They put resources toward their objectives rather than profits. They interact and accomplish through engaging volunteers, recruiting supporters, and accessing financing possibilities. Starting a nonprofit allows for personal fulfillment and the alignment of your ideals and professional interests. It is a satisfying undertaking that allows us to contribute to the greater good and strive towards a better society.

This book will take you on a journey to better understand nonprofit enterprises. Discover the power of nonprofit influence, grasp the legal issues, and learn how to construct a sustainable organization. Read about program administration, financial sustainability, governance, and ethical issues. Investigate evaluation and impact assessment, organizational growth, and leadership development as they occur throughout a nonprofit. Whether you read this book cover to cover, or you focus on sections of interest, it should connect you with the information and resources you need to maintain influence, embrace change, and celebrate accomplishments on your never-ending path to make a difference.

Without much ado, onward we go!!

CHAPTER 1:

NON-PROFIT BUSINESSES/ORGANIZATIONS [THE BASICS]

Why Start a Nonprofit Business/Organization?

In today's complicated world, there are many reasons why founding a charity business may be a fascinating and satisfying endeavor. Any one of them could be the spark that starts a new nonprofit organization.

Purpose-driven Mission: Nonprofit organizations are driven by a keen sense of purpose. They seek to solve societal problems, empower underprivileged individuals or groups, and contribute to the greater good. For example, imagine a small literacy group that begins with a handful of volunteers hosting weekend reading circles in a park. Within two years, it grows into an after-school program serving hundreds of children. This shows that even modest beginnings can unite a community around a shared cause. A defined purpose provides nonprofits with direction and helps them unite supporters, volunteers, and contributors around a shared mission.

Making a difference: Nonprofits provide a platform for positive change and the resolution of important social and environmental concerns. They can directly touch the lives of individuals and work toward systemic reforms by focusing on specific problems or localities. Picture a coastal cleanup effort that starts as one small community event and eventually becomes a regional network advocating for stronger environmental protections. This opportunity to influence substantial change is frequently cited as a major reason for starting a charity.

Unmet needs: Nonprofits have the freedom to identify and address a multitude of unmet societal needs. They can fill gaps where government or for-profit organizations may be unable to devote adequate money or attention. Think of a rural food pantry delivering fresh produce to seniors who live far from the nearest grocery store, a service no commercial business finds profitable, yet essential to the people it reaches. By identifying underserved communities and implementing creative solutions, nonprofits can have a direct and immediate impact.

Recruiting volunteers and supporters: Nonprofits often attract passionate people who want to make a difference. Many foster a sense of community and shared purpose by offering opportunities for involvement as volunteers, board members, or advocates. Imagine an animal rescue that operates entirely through volunteers who foster pets until they are adopted into permanent homes. This involvement promotes teamwork, sparks creativity, and builds a network of people dedicated to the organization's mission.

Tax benefits and funding opportunities: Nonprofit organizations can benefit from specific tax exemptions, helping them reduce operational costs and direct more resources toward their initiatives. They also have access to a wider variety of funding options, including grants, donations, and partnerships. For instance, a local conservation nonprofit might sustain its programs through a mix of state environmental grants and collaborations with outdoor equipment companies. These financial resources help sustain and expand the organization's impact over time.

Personal fulfillment: For many, establishing a nonprofit is deeply rewarding. It allows them to align personal values with professional endeavors and see the impact of their work firsthand. Consider the founder of a youth arts program who watches students perform for the first time, describing it as the proudest moment of their career. The opportunity to witness transformation in the lives of others can be profoundly satisfying.

Collaboration and collective impact: To address complex issues, nonprofits often partner with local or national organizations, government agencies, and other entities. By combining resources, skills, and influence, they can achieve more together. Picture several housing organizations joining forces to build an affordable apartment complex that none could have completed alone. Such collaboration results in more comprehensive solutions, greater efficiency, and a stronger ability to create long-term change.

Starting a nonprofit organization provides a unique chance to address social and environmental issues, inspire positive change, and have a lasting influence. It blends purpose, passion, and the ability to unite communities behind a shared vision of a better future.

Understanding Nonprofit Organizations

Nonprofits, also known as not-for-profit organizations, play an important role in solving social issues and serving the public interest. These groups work in diverse fields, motivated by the desire to make a positive difference in society. Charities, foundations, associations, social enterprises, and community-based groups are all examples of nonprofits.

The primary difference between nonprofits and for-profit organizations is their mission. While for-profits aim to maximize returns for owners, nonprofits prioritize societal improvement and the achievement of specific social or environmental goals. For instance, a commercial tutoring company may charge by the hour, while a nonprofit literacy program might offer lessons free of charge, funded entirely through grants and donations. This mission-first approach allows nonprofits to focus on areas that governments or businesses might overlook.

Nonprofits rely heavily on donations and grants from individuals, businesses, foundations, and government sources. These resources are vital for delivering services, conducting research, lobbying for policy change, and developing innovative solutions to community challenges.

The nonprofit sector is a powerful driver of social impact and positive change. Understanding their structure and funding needs helps reveal both the opportunities and challenges nonprofits face in creating lasting benefits.

The Power of Nonprofit Impact

Nonprofits, unlike many government or business efforts, have the agility and commitment to address challenges that might otherwise be ignored. They operate with a strong dedication to social causes and community well-being.

They often provide essential services for underserved communities. Imagine a community coding program that offers free classes to unemployed adults, giving them skills to find work in the technology sector and provide for their families. Nonprofits empower individuals by equipping them with the tools and support they need to overcome obstacles and succeed.

Their influence also extends to advocacy. Picture a coalition of environmental groups successfully lobbying for renewable energy policies that reshape local energy production for decades to come. These organizations challenge the status quo, pushing for justice, equality, and sustainability while tackling issues like poverty, discrimination, and environmental decline.

Through awareness campaigns, community events, and advocacy work, nonprofits encourage people from all walks of life to join their mission. Volunteers, donors, and beneficiaries become active partners in change, creating a ripple effect that extends far beyond the initial project.

Overview of the Book

Welcome to a practical and engaging guide for founding a nonprofit business, organization, charity, or project. Whether you have a passion for a particular cause, want to improve your neighborhood, or aim to address a major societal challenge, this book is your roadmap to success.

Each chapter covers an essential aspect of building and sustaining a nonprofit, from defining your mission and vision to navigating legal requirements, raising funds, building a team, creating programs, measuring impact, and sustaining growth.

Real-world scenarios, leadership tips, and best practices will help bring these concepts to life. You'll see how nonprofits can start from a kitchen table, a coffee shop meeting, or even a single social media post and still grow into a force for change.

This journey is not meant to be taken alone. Throughout these pages, you'll discover tools, resources, and networks that can help you launch and strengthen your organization.

Take a deep breath, embrace the possibilities, and prepare to explore the power of creating a nonprofit. By the end of this book, you'll have the confidence and knowledge to lead an organization that can make a meaningful and lasting difference.

CHAPTER 2:

DEFINING YOUR MISSION AND VISION

Crafting a Mission Statement

Crafting a mission statement is a pivotal first step in the journey of starting a nonprofit business. Your mission statement serves as a beacon, guiding your organization's purpose and goals. It encapsulates the essence of your work and the change you aspire to create. There are a number of overarching elements which often coalesce to form the basis of an organization's final mission statement.

Core Values: Identify the core values that will drive your organiza-tion's actions and decisions. These values should reflect the principles and beliefs at the heart of your cause. They provide a moral compass for your nonprofit.

Specificity: Clearly define the issue or cause your nonprofit aims to address. Be specific about the population or community you intend to serve. This clarity helps potential supporters, donors, and volunteers understand the focus of your work and connect with your mission.

Impact: Articulate the specific impact or outcomes your organization seeks to achieve. Describe the positive change you envision in the lives of individuals, communities, or the broader society. This clarifies the purpose of your nonprofit and helps stakeholders understand the difference you aim to make.

Uniqueness: Highlight what sets your organization apart from others working in the same field. Emphasize your unique approach, perspective, or methodology. For example, two nonprofits might both address youth homelessness, but one could focus on long-term housing and job training while the other offers rapid-response shelters and mental health services. Both share a cause, yet their mission statements reflect very different approaches. Showcasing your distinctive method helps you stand out and attract support.

Inspirational Language: Use language that resonates with your target audience and stakeholders. Choose words that inspire and evoke emotions. Your mission statement should ignite passion, create a sense of purpose, and inspire people to rally behind your cause.

Authenticity: Aim for a mission statement that is concise, ideally one or two sentences long. This simplicity makes it easy to communicate, remember, and share with others. Also consider incorporating your own unique ideas and perspectives into your mission statement. Your personal touch will infuse it with authenticity and make it a true reflection of your organization's values and aspirations.

Crafting a compelling mission statement is a transformative process. It shapes the identity of your nonprofit and lays the foundation for your impactful journey ahead. Let your mission statement become a rallying cry that inspires action and fuels the passion of all who encounter it.

Identifying Your Target Population

To effectively address a problem or cause, it is crucial to identify and understand the target population your nonprofit will serve. Your target population refers to the specific group or community that will benefit from your organization's programs, services, or advocacy. Here are key considerations when identifying your target population:

Needs and Gaps: Start by identifying the specific needs and gaps that exist within the target population. Conduct thorough research, engage with potential beneficiaries, and listen to their voices. For instance, a nonprofit exploring after-school programs might discover through community interviews that parents value free tutoring more than sports activities, prompting a shift in the program's focus. Understanding their needs is essential for developing relevant and impactful programs and services.

Demographics: Gain a deep understanding of the demographic characteristics of your target population. Consider factors such as age, gender, ethnicity, socio-economic background, education level, or geographic location. These demographics influence the unique challenges and circumstances that your nonprofit will address. Tailoring your programs and services to their specific needs will increase their relevance and effectiveness.

Accessibility: Evaluate the accessibility of your services to the target population. Identify any barriers they might face in accessing your organization's offerings. Consider factors such as language barriers, transportation limitations, cultural sensitivities, or technological constraints. By recognizing and addressing these barriers, you can ensure that your services are accessible and inclusive.

Stakeholder Engagement: Involve the target population and other relevant stakeholders in the process of defining your organization's mission, vision, and programs whenever possible. Engage them in meaningful dialogue and seek their input. By involving the target population and other stakeholders, you can gain valuable perspectives and ensure that your nonprofit's work is aligned with their needs and aspirations. This collaborative approach enhances the relevance and impact of your initiatives.

Additionally, recognize the diversity and individuality within the target population you hope to serve, as well as the intersecting factors that shape their experiences. By embracing a holistic and inclusive approach, you can create programs and services that address their multifaceted needs and promote meaningful change.

Understanding your target population is fundamental to the success of your nonprofit. By gaining a full awareness of their needs, demographics, accessibility challenges, and engaging them as stakeholders, you can develop impactful initiatives that make a positive difference in their lives and drive lasting social change.

Aligning Your Goals with Your Mission and Vision

Once you have a clear mission and vision, it is crucial to align your goals with them. Your goals should be Specific, Measurable, Attainable, Relevant, and Time-bound (SMART). They serve as stepping stones toward achieving your mission and vision. Here are key considerations when aligning your goals:

Impact-oriented: Ensure that your goals are directly linked to the impact you want to create. Align them with the outcomes and objectives outlined in your mission and vision statements. For example, if your mission is to improve access to education, your goals may include increasing enrollment rates, expanding scholarship programs, or reducing dropout rates. Keep the focus on the ultimate impact you aim to achieve.

Prioritization: Determine which goals are most critical and prioritize them accordingly. Focus on goals that will have the most significant impact on your mission and vision. Conduct a SWOT (Strengths, Weaknesses, Opportunities, Threats) analysis to identify areas that require immediate attention. For instance, a community arts nonprofit might find in its SWOT analysis that a strength is a highly skilled volunteer base, a weakness is limited performance space, an opportunity is a potential partnership with the local library, and a threat is a new arts center competing for grants. (See the sample SWOT analysis in chapter 3 for a visual example of how you can organize your own.)

Breakdown and Milestones: Break down your goals into smaller, manageable milestones. This approach makes them more attainable and allows for regular progress monitoring. Define specific targets or outcomes for each milestone. Celebrate achievements along the way to maintain motivation and momentum.

Collaboration: Involve your team members, stakeholders, and beneficiaries in the goal-setting process. This collaborative approach fosters ownership, commitment, and shared responsibility. Engage stakeholders to gain diverse perspectives and ensure that your goals reflect the needs and aspirations of those you serve.

Resource Alignment: Evaluate the resources needed to achieve each goal. This includes financial resources, human resources, infrastructure, and partnerships. Ensure that your organization has the necessary resources and strategies in place to support the pursuit of your goals. Effective resource allocation is vital for successful goal attainment.

Monitoring and Evaluation: Develop a system for tracking progress and evaluating the effectiveness of your goals. Regularly assess whether your strategies are yielding the desired outcomes. Establish metrics and indicators to measure progress. Recognize that goals are not set in stone and can be revised as your nonprofit evolves and learns. Regularly revisit and reassess your goals to ensure they remain aligned with your organization's purpose and adapt to new challenges and opportunities.

By aligning your goals with your mission and vision, you provide a clear roadmap for decision-making, resource allocation, and program development. This alignment ensures that your organization's efforts are focused, purposeful, and directed toward achieving the desired impact.

CHAPTER 3:

CONDUCTING MARKET RESEARCH

Understanding the Nonprofit Landscape

Before embarking on starting a nonprofit business, it is crucial to gain a comprehensive understanding of the nonprofit landscape related to your cause or issue. This involves conducting research to identify existing organizations, initiatives, and programs that are already addressing similar or related problems. Understanding the existing landscape will help you identify gaps, potential collaborators, and opportunities for collaboration. There are several key considerations when researching the nonprofit landscape in order to appropriately enter the space.

Identify Key Players: Start by identifying prominent nonprofit organizations and initiatives that are working in your field. Learn as much as you can about their missions, programs, target populations, impact, and geographic scope. This knowledge will provide valuable insights into their strengths, areas of focus, and potential areas for collaboration or differentiation. For example, if you are planning to open a community arts center, you might find that while several nearby organizations run weekend workshops, none offer weekday after-school programs for teens. This may be an opening your nonprofit could fill. By understanding the key players, you can better position your organization within the broader nonprofit ecosystem.

Assess the Competitive Landscape: Identify direct competitors, such as entities that are working on similar issues or addressing the same target population. Analyze their strategies, approaches, and impact. This analysis will help you understand their strengths and weaknesses, enabling you to identify unique opportunities or gaps that your nonprofit can address or where you could partner. A new literacy nonprofit, for instance, might discover that existing programs in their city focus on young children, leaving few options for adults seeking to improve reading skills for career advancement. By understanding the competitive landscape, you can find ways to differentiate your organization and offer innovative solutions.

Study Successful Nonprofits: Take the time to study successful nonprofit organizations that have achieved significant impact in your field. Analyze their strategies, fundraising approaches, program models, and partnerships. Learn from their best practices and successes, adapting them to suit your organization's unique context. For example, if you are launching an environmental cleanup group, you might model your volunteer engagement strategy after a coastal conservation nonprofit that doubled participation by pairing clean-up events with community festivals. Studying successful nonprofits can provide valuable insights and inspiration for your own organization's development and growth.

While you are learning about the other organizations that share your nonprofit's space, you can look for trends, emerging issues, and potential areas for collaboration or innovation. By gaining a comprehensive understanding of the nonprofit landscape, you can position your organization strategically, identify areas where you can contribute effectively, and maximize your potential for impact.

Remember, this research is an ongoing process. As the nonprofit landscape evolves, continue to stay informed and adapt your strategies accordingly. By staying connected and aware of the larger ecosystem, you can navigate challenges, forge valuable partnerships, and contribute meaningfully to your cause or issue.

Identifying Community Needs and Gaps

Thorough study and analysis are required to answer community needs successfully. This method entails actively interacting with the target population, stakeholders, and community members to understand their needs, issues, and goals. Understanding the gaps and unmet requirements allows you to build programs and services that directly target those areas.

Conduct Surveys and Interviews: Create surveys or conduct interviews to acquire quantitative and qualitative data on the community's needs and difficulties. Engage with those who are directly touched by the issue, as well as important stakeholders and community leaders. For example, a group considering a youth mentorship program might find through interviews that the greatest local concern is not career guidance, but access to safe transportation for students. This may prompt the nonprofit to design a mentorship program that also provides travel support. You may acquire insights into the community's particular needs, objectives, and opinions by gathering data through surveys and interviews.

Examine Existing Research, Reports, and Studies: Examine existing research, reports, and studies linked to the topic or target population. Government reports, academic studies, and community evaluations can all give useful information and insights. You can comprehend the context, detect patterns, and evaluate community requirements by examining existing data and reports.

Community Listening Sessions: Hold community listening sessions or focus groups to actively engage people of the community. Make a secure atmosphere for open discourse in which individuals may express their experiences, concerns, and ideas. This direct information from community members will give greater insights into the community's needs and goals. For instance, a neighborhood safety nonprofit might learn during a listening session that residents are more concerned about lighting and walkability than additional police presence, shifting the focus of the nonprofit's first project.

Community Organization Partnerships: Collaborate with local community groups, NGOs, and social service agencies to obtain a better knowledge of community needs. Use their knowledge, networks, and experience to help you with your study. Engaging with existing groups can also help you develop ties with community leaders and get insights. If you're planning a food security project, a local food pantry might share data revealing which neighborhoods face the highest rates of grocery store closures, guiding your choice of service area.

Meet with local players and leaders in your area and ask about what needs they see. Being present in the community while actively listening and watching might give vital insights into community needs that typical research approaches may not capture. Remember that community needs might change over time, therefore it's critical to keep an ongoing communication with the community. Reassess and update your understanding of community needs on a regular basis to ensure your programs and services remain relevant and meaningful.

Analyzing Competitors and Collaborators

Analyzing both competitors and potential collaborators is crucial for the success of your nonprofit. By understanding the strengths, weaknesses, and approaches of similar organizations, you can identify opportunities for collaboration, differentiation, and innovation. Below are four considerations while analyzing competitors and collaborators.

SWOT Analysis: Conduct a SWOT (Strengths, Weaknesses, Oppor-tunities, Threats) analysis of competing nonprofits. Identify their strengths and weaknesses, such as program effectiveness, financial stability, partnerships, and marketing strategies. Assess the opportunities and threats they may pose to your organization. This analysis will help you identify areas where your nonprofit can excel or fill gaps. This can be done with a simple diagram or chart, and will help you to see different aspects of your project all in one place. (See the sample SWOT analysis image for an example of how you could do one.)

STRENGTHS	WEAKNESSES
• Strong brand recognition • Skilled workforce • Efficient processes	• Limited financial resources • High employee turnover • Outdated technology
OPPORTUNITIES	**THREATS**
• Market growth • Emerging technologies • Strategic partnerships	• Increasing competition • Economic dowturnns • Changing regulations

Collaboration Opportunities: Identify potential partners and collaborators whose missions and values align with your organization. Explore opportunities for joint programs, shared resources, and collective impact. For example, a mental health nonprofit might work with a local library to host wellness workshops, combining expertise with a free, accessible venue. Collaboration can enhance your effectiveness, expand your reach, and amplify your impact. Look for organizations that complement your work and share a common goal, and consider how you can work together to achieve mutual benefits.

Differentiation Strategies: Determine how your nonprofit can differentiate itself from competitors. Consider your unique approach, innovative programs or services, specialized expertise, or distinct target population. Highlight what sets your organization apart and how it can attract supporters, donors, and volunteers who resonate with your unique value proposition. Emphasize the aspects that make your organization stand out and provide added value to the community.

Gap Analysis: Identify gaps or unmet needs within the existing nonprofit landscape. Assess whether there are underserved populations or specific aspects of the issue that are not adequately addressed by current organizations. This analysis will help you identify niche areas where your nonprofit can make a significant impact. By focusing on unmet needs, you can position your organization as a valuable contributor in the field.

Additionally, consider staying updated on emerging trends, innovative approaches, and best practices within your sector. Attend conferences, engage with professional networks, and stay connected to the latest research and developments. By being proactive in your industry, you can adapt and respond to changing needs and leverage opportunities for growth and collaboration. Remember, competition and collaboration can coexist. By understanding the nonprofit landscape and strategically positioning your organization, you can find ways to work with others to maximize impact and ultimately achieve your mission.

Assessing Funding and Resource Availability

To sustain your nonprofit business, it is crucial to assess the availability of funding and resources within the sector. Understanding the funding landscape will help you develop effective fundraising strategies and identify potential sources of financial support.

Funding Sources: Explore the various funding sources available to nonprofit organizations, such as grants, donations, sponsorships, and fundraising events. Identify foundations, government programs, corporate social responsibility initiatives, and individual donors who have a vested interest in your cause. For instance, a youth music program might combine small business sponsorships with annual benefit concerts to keep programming free for participants. Diversifying your funding sources can help mitigate risks and ensure stability over time.

Grant Opportunities: Investigate grant opportunities that align with your mission and programs. Explore national, regional, and local grant-making organizations that provide funding for nonprofit initiatives. Familiarize yourself with their funding criteria, application processes, and reporting requirements. Develop a compelling case for support that effectively communicates the impact of your work.

Resource Partnerships: Identify potential resource partners, such as corporations, businesses, or other nonprofits, that can provide in-kind support or resources. This may include pro bono services, donated goods, access to facilities or equipment, or technical expertise. For example, a health education nonprofit might partner with a local printer to produce brochures at no cost, freeing up budget for additional outreach. Building strategic partnerships can help alleviate some of the resource challenges faced by your nonprofit and expand your reach.

Volunteer Engagement: Assess the availability of volunteers who are passionate about your cause. Determine the interest and capacity of individuals and groups who are willing to contribute their time and skills to support your organization's mission. Volunteer engagement can supplement your human resource needs and expand your reach in the community. Develop volunteer management strategies to attract, retain, and recognize volunteers effectively.

Economic Trends: Stay informed about economic trends and changes that may affect the availability of funding and resources. Monitor shifts in government priorities, philanthropic trends, and donor preferences to adapt your fundraising strategies accordingly. Stay proactive and responsive to changes in the external environment.

Sustainability Planning: Develop a comprehensive sustainability plan that outlines your long-term financial and resource strategies. This plan should include strategies for diversifying funding sources, cultivating donor relationships, building an endowment or reserve fund, and fostering a culture of philanthropy within your organization. (See chapter 8 for more on this topic)

CHAPTER 4:
LEGAL CONSIDERATIONS FOR NONPROFIT BUSINESSES

Legal Structures for Nonprofit Organizations

It is critical to understand the various legal structures available before starting a nonprofit business. Your legal structure will be determined by elements such as your objective, operations, governance structure, and tax-exempt status. The most popular structures for nonprofit endeavors are outlined below.

Unincorporated Association: This is the most basic type of nonprofit organization. It is a loose collection of people that gather together for a shared goal. While it provides flexibility, an unincorporated group may not have independent legal standing or liability protection. It is vital to emphasize that without a distinct legal body, personal liability for the organization's conduct may extend to its participants. For example, a small neighborhood gardening group might operate informally for years, but if a participant is injured during a volunteer event, the organizers could be held personally liable.

Charitable Trust: A charitable trust is formed when assets are committed to philanthropic causes. It is governed by trustees who are accountable for achieving the trust's goals. Charitable trusts are governed by various state laws and regulations. Trusts have significant benefits in terms of asset management and eternal life, but they may also have more complex administration responsibilities.

Limited Liability Company (LLC): While typically associated with for-profit enterprises, several jurisdictions enable nonprofit LLCs to be formed through the filing of Articles of Organization with the host state. Nonprofit limited liability companies (LLCs) offer management and tax flexibility. They blend some of an LLC's operational freedom with some of a corporation's limited liability protection. Nonprofit LLCs, however, may not be recognized in all states, therefore it is critical to investigate the legal requirements in your area.

Nonprofit Corporation: A nonprofit corporation is a separate legal organization that offers its members and directors limited liability protection. It necessitates submitting Articles of Incorporation with the relevant state agency as well as following to specified governance and reporting standards. By incorporating, the group receives legal status, allowing it to enter into contracts, possess property, and take legal action on its own behalf. For instance, a youth theater program might incorporate so it can rent performance space under the organization's name, apply for grants that require formal legal status, and protect its board members from personal liability.

Fiscal Sponsorship: Fiscal sponsorship is an agreement in which an existing nonprofit organization (the sponsor) offers administrative, legal, and financial control to a project or program that lacks its own nonprofit status. The sponsor acts as the fiscal agent, ensuring that all legal and reporting obligations

24

are met. Fiscal sponsorship might be a temporary option for organizations that are just getting started or working on specific initiatives.

To identify the most appropriate legal form for your nonprofit business, contact with legal specialists that specialize in nonprofit law and examine state legislation. They may offer advice based on your individual circumstances and ensure that all legal and regulatory obligations are met. When making your selection, consider considerations like as liability protection, governance structure, tax ramifications, and the potential to attract money and grants.

Obtaining Tax-Exempt Status

One of the primary benefits of establishing a nonprofit organization is the possibility of obtaining tax-exempt status, which allows your organization to accept tax-deductible donations and various exemptions from federal and state taxes. Consider the following procedures to get tax-exempt status:

Eligibility: Review the tax-exempt qualifying standards which are found in IRS code 501. For example, organizations founded and run only for charitable, educational, religious, scientific, or literary purposes may qualify for tax-exempt status under Internal Revenue Code section 501(c)(3). A community literacy nonprofit, for example, could qualify under the educational category if its programs focus entirely on free tutoring and reading programs for underserved populations.

Creating a Nonprofit Organization: Create a nonprofit organization by submitting articles of incorporation or other relevant documents with the appropriate state agency, if you haven't already. Make sure that they contain the appropriate language to qualify for tax-exempt status.

Applying for Tax-Exempt Status: Complete and submit Form 1023 or Form 1023-EZ (Application for Recognition of Exemption) to the IRS, together with the necessary papers and filing costs. Providing extensive information about your organization's activities, governance structure, finances, and proposed projects is required throughout the application process.

State Tax-Exempt Status: Depending on your state, you may be required to apply separately for state tax-exempt status. To guarantee compliance with state tax laws, research the rules and processes of your state's taxation body.

Compliance and Reporting: Once you have obtained tax-exempt status, you must adhere to continuous reporting and filing obligations. This involves submitting yearly information reports with the IRS, such as Form 990 or 990-EZ, as well as any state-specific reporting requirements. Keep track of the deadlines and reporting requirements to keep your tax-exempt status. There may also be laws in your jurisdiction related to exempt status or soliciting donations.

It is recommended to obtain advice from legal and accounting specialists who specialize in nonprofit law to ensure that all necessary stages are completed correctly and in accordance with applicable laws and regulations. They may help you negotiate the complexity of tax-exempt status and give crucial support throughout the application process. You will have the best luck in this step if you collect all the required information for your professional and bring it to your first meeting.

Governance and Legal Compliance

To preserve their tax-exempt status and guarantee responsible operations, nonprofit organizations must adhere to strict governance and legal compliance standards. Take into account the following governance and compliance issues:

Board of Directors: Form a board of directors that will be in charge of the organization's governance and strategic direction. Ensure that the board is made up of people who are dedicated to the organization's goal and have a wide range of skills and knowledge. Encourage active engagement, ethical behavior, and a strong responsibility culture. Most states require at least three directors for an organization. For example, a small environmental nonprofit might recruit a local attorney, an accountant, and a community organizer to ensure legal, financial, and grassroots expertise are represented on the board.

Bylaws and Policies: Create thorough bylaws outlining the governance, decision-making, and board operations norms and processes. Draft rules and processes for dealing with conflicts of interest, financial management, fundraising, and program administration. These documents serve as a roadmap for your organization's activities and assure legal compliance.

Financial Management: Maintain openness and accountability by using strong financial management procedures. Establishing internal controls, performing frequent financial audits, and maintaining correct financial records are all part of this. Follow accounting standards and financial reporting regulations. Create a budgeting approach that is in line with the strategic aims of your firm.

Reporting and Disclosure: Nonprofits must be transparent to its stakeholders and the general public. Create an annual report that displays your organization's achievements, impact, and financial data. File yearly information returns with the IRS, such as Form 990, and guarantee timely compliance. To communicate vital organizational information, consider developing a public transparency page on your website to share annual reporting information.

Law and Regulation Compliance: Stay current on federal, state, and local rules and regulations that apply to nonprofit organizations. Comply with all applicable employment laws, intellectual property rights, privacy rules, and other legal obligations. Engage legal advice as needed to assure compliance and reduce risks. Work to create an organizational culture of ethical behavior and honesty.

Fundraising Regulations: Understand and follow fundraising restrictions, such as solicitation laws, charitable registration requirements, and reporting duties. Different jurisdictions may have different requirements, so be informed with the rules in the locations where you operate. Ensure that your fundraising techniques are transparent, polite, and in accordance with ethical standards.

Risk Management: Implement risk management procedures to detect, analyze, and reduce possible hazards to your nonprofit. Conduct a risk assessment to identify weaknesses and establish ways to mitigate them. Create policies for insurance coverage, cybersecurity, data protection, and crisis response. Review and update your risk management strategies on a regular basis to reflect new risks and changes in the operational environment.

Annual Filings and Renewals: File yearly reports, renewals, and other needed papers with the proper government authorities to retain legal and tax-exempt status. Keep track of filing deadlines and report requirements. Create a procedure to ensure timely reporting and prevent potential penalties or loss of tax-exempt status. This can be done electronically or even on a paper calendar.

To guarantee that your organization stays in compliance with the ever-changing legal landscape, seek advice from legal and accounting specialists with expertise in nonprofit law. Review and update your governance and compliance policies on a regular basis to react to changes and maintain the long-term profitability and sustainability of your nonprofit organization.

Legal Compliance in International Operations

When engaging in international operations, nonprofit organizations need to navigate the legal and regulatory frameworks of different countries. Below are some points to consider if you are interested in working or collaborating internationally.

Cultural Competence: Enhance your cultural competence to effectively connect with and engage diverse communities and stakeholders. Understand local customs, traditions, and communication styles. Adapting your approach and programs to the cultural context can enhance the effectiveness and sustainability of your international operations.

Local Partnerships and Networks: Establish partnerships with local organizations, community leaders, and networks to gain insights into the local context and navigate regulatory requirements. Local partners in a foreign community can provide valuable guidance, connections, and on-the-ground support for a multinational initiative. For instance, a medical outreach nonprofit might work with a village health committee to arrange clinic schedules that align with local market days so residents can attend without losing income.

Compliance with International Laws and Treaties: Familiarize yourself with international laws and treaties relevant to your organization's activities, such as human rights conventions, environmental agreements, and international labor standards. Ensure your operations align with these legal frameworks and commitments. If necessary, legal support is your friend here.

Due Diligence and Risk Assessment: Conduct thorough due diligence and risk assessments when engaging in international activities. Assess potential risks associated with political instability, security concerns, legal barriers, and reputational risks. Develop risk management strategies to mitigate these risks and ensure the safety and security of your staff and beneficiaries. This includes organizational transparency of all plans related to safety of goods and personnel.

Local Staffing and Employment Practices: Comply with local labor laws and regulations when hiring staff or engaging volunteers internationally. Understand the legal requirements related to contracts, wages, working conditions, and social security contributions. Consider engaging local human resources expertise to ensure compliance with local employment laws wherever your employees will be working.

Financial Compliance and Transparency: Understand international financial regulations and reporting requirements. Comply with international accounting standards, cross-border transaction regulations, and foreign currency exchange laws. Maintain accurate and transparent financial records to demonstrate accountability and compliance.

Local Stakeholder Engagement: Engage with local communities and stakeholders to ensure your activities align with their needs, aspirations, and priorities. Foster meaningful partnerships and involve local stakeholders in decision-making processes to ensure sustainability and local ownership of initiatives, whether independent or with international partners.

Continuous Learning and Adaptation: Embrace a learning mindset and be open to adapting your strategies and approaches based on local feedback and experiences. Regularly evaluate the impact and effective-ness of your international programs and make necessary adjustments to improve outcomes. Keep in mind that what works in your local municipalities may not work in another.

International operations require a nuanced understanding of legal, cultural, and operational aspects. Seek guidance from international nonprofit experts, local advisors, and legal professionals with experience in international law and cross-border operations. This will help ensure that your organization operates in compliance with local regulations and makes a positive and sustainable impact in the communities you serve.

CHAPTER 5:

BUILDING A VIABLE NONPROFIT BUSINESS

Developing a Project Plan

Developing a strategic plan for a program or project is like charting a course for your nonprofit, setting direction toward success and lasting impact. Each project plan connects back to the larger strategic vision, ensuring your organization stays aligned with its mission and remains viable. The following steps will help you craft a plan that engages your team, inspires stakeholders, and drives meaningful results.

Project Vision: Imagine your nonprofit as a hero on a noble quest. Define a clear and inspiring vision that encapsulates your purpose and fuels your major projects. Craft a compelling vision statement that paints a vivid picture of the positive change you aspire to create in the world. You will reference your overall mission here to maintain a cohesive overall direction. For example, a neighborhood arts nonprofit might envision a future where every child has access to free creative workshops, using that vision to guide each program they design.

Goals and Objectives: Picture your goals as shining beacons on the horizon, guiding your organization forward. Set SMART goals that are Specific, Measurable, Attainable, Relevant, and Time-bound. Break them down into bite-sized objectives that serve as stepping stones for your projects, just as you did for your organization as a whole.

SWOT Analysis: Unleash your inner detective and conduct a SWOT analysis. Discover your organization's hidden strengths that set you apart, pinpoint any weaknesses that need attention, uncover opportunities to seize, and identify threats that may lurk in the shadows. Armed with this knowledge, you can craft strategies specific for each of your projects just as you did for the organization as a whole. (See sample SWOT analysis image in chapter 3 for a visual example.)

Strategies and Action Plans: Imagine your project plan as a treasure map, leading you to your goals. Explore innovative program development ideas, craft compelling fundraising strategies, devise captivating marketing and communication plans, seek out valuable partnerships, and plan for the growth and development of each major project depending on each project's need. Create action plans that break down each project into actionable steps, assign responsibilities to your team and set deadlines that keep everyone motivated. For instance, a food pantry launching a home delivery service might assign mapping routes to one volunteer, social media promotion to another, and partnership outreach to a staff member, with each milestone tracked weekly.

Monitoring and Evaluation: Picture yourself as a captain navigating the treacherous waters of the nonprofit landscape. Define key performance indicators that will serve as your project compass, helping you track progress and stay on course. Regularly review your project's performance, celebrate victories, learn from challenges, and adapt your strategies to ensure you're always moving in the right direction. Keep track of what worked (and what didn't) to benefit your next project!

Fundraising and Resource Mobilization

Welcome to the thrilling world of fundraising and resource mobilization! Get ready to embark on a journey that will propel your nonprofit to new heights. Here are some strategies to help you conquer the realm of fundraising.

Individual Donations: Imagine each individual donor as a superhero, ready to join forces with your cause. Cultivate personal connections by understanding their passions and motivations. Develop a dynamic donor engagement plan that includes tailored communication, heartfelt gratitude, and impactful stories of how their support makes a difference. Harness the power of online fundraising platforms, launch compelling direct mail campaigns, and employ major donor cultivation techniques to attract and retain these superhero supporters. For example, a youth mentorship nonprofit might send a quarterly "impact snapshot" email to donors, highlighting one student's success story to show tangible results.

Grant Writing and Proposals: Sharpen your grant-seeking sword and delve into the realm of foundations, government agencies, and corporate giving programs. Research opportunities that align with your mission and craft goal-oriented grant proposals. Weave a captivating narrative that clearly showcases your organization's purpose, goals, innovative programs, and expected impact. Forge relationships with program officers, engaging them in conversations about your work and following up diligently on grant applications. Make sure you have support for grant tracking and compliance should you be awarded funding.

Corporate Partnerships: Summon the strength of corporate allies to amplify your impact. Seek partnerships with corporations that share your values and passion. Explore sponsorship opportunities that bring mutual benefits, such as brand exposure and community engagement. Craft compelling proposals that highlight the transformative power of collaboration. Tap into the realm of cause-related marketing, where the purchase of products or services can directly support your organization's mission.

Events and Fundraisers: Unleash your creativity and organize enchanting fundraising events that captivate supporters. Imagine galas that transport attendees to a magical world, charity auctions where treasures are won in the name of a good cause, walkathons that unite communities, and online crowdfunding campaigns that inspire a global movement. Promote these events with enthusiasm, utilizing social media, traditional marketing channels, and the power of word-of-mouth.

Earned Income Strategies: Channel your entrepreneurial spirit and explore innovative ways to generate direct revenue. Leverage your organization's expertise and skills to offer fee-based services, develop unique products, or establish social enterprises. By diversifying your income streams, you not only generate funds but also increase your organization's sustainability and impact.

Planned Giving: Unlock the realm of legacy gifts and weave a tapestry of lasting impact. Educate your supporters about the significance of including your organization in their estate plans and wills. Develop a comprehensive planned giving program that empowers them to leave a lasting legacy. Provide personalized guidance, resources, and recognition to honor these supporters who have chosen to support your cause beyond their lifetime.

Traditional Third-Party Marketing: Engage the expertise of an established marketing or fundraising firm to design and execute a professional campaign on your behalf. These firms bring specialized skills, networks, and proven strategies to amplify your message, often managing everything from creative development and media placement to direct mail, email outreach, and donor acquisition programs. Similar to how some health charities contract with professional agencies to run seasonal giving drives or national awareness campaigns, this approach can allow your team to focus on mission delivery while the campaign logistics are handled externally.

Now, with these strategies in hand, go forth and develop your cause in the fundraising realm. Embrace the adventure, adapt your approach, and remember that each supporter and every dollar raised brings you closer to realizing your nonprofit's mission. The journey may be challenging, but with passion, creativity, and resilience, you can create a sustainable future and change lives for the better.

Building Partnerships and Collaboration

Welcome to the world of collaboration and strategic partnerships, where the possibilities are endless and the impact is boundless. Prepare to embark on an exciting journey of shared goals and collective action. Here's a guide to help you navigate this captivating part of the task:

Identify Potential Partners: Cast your gaze upon the local community and identify organizations, groups, and stakeholders whose paths intersect with yours. Seek out those who share similar goals or possess complementary strengths. Explore opportunities to combine forces and unlock the power of collaboration, even if that means starting in a supporting role. For example, a local literacy nonprofit might team up with a housing assistance program to provide reading workshops at community centers, reaching audiences neither could reach alone.

Assess Alignment: Peer through the lens of alignment to determine if potential partners are a perfect match. Consider their track record, reputation, and capacity to contribute. Look for shared values, a common purpose, and a genuine willingness to collaborate.

Establish Clear Objectives: Carve a clear path forward by defining the objectives and expected outcomes of the partnership. Paint a shared vision and set ambitious goals that align with the mission and strategic priorities of all involved. Ensure that everyone understands their roles, responsibilities, and the resources they bring to the table.

Collaborative Projects and Programs: Dive into the realm of collaborative projects and programs, where magic happens when minds intertwine. Identify specific initiatives where collaboration can unleash extraordinary change. Craft joint ventures that harness the unique strengths and resources of each partner. Establish communication channels that flow like rivers, decision-making processes that sparkle with clarity, and accountability mechanisms that stand firm.

Resource Sharing: Imagine a treasure library where resources are shared and multiplied. Explore opportunities to pool your collective resources, whether it's facilities, equipment, expertise, or networks. By sharing, you unlock new dimensions of efficiency, reduce costs, and maximize the reach and depth of your impact.

Advocacy and Policy Initiatives: Unite your voices and march toward the halls of power. Collaborate with other organizations to advocate for policy changes and systemic solutions that address the root causes of the issues you are passionate about.

Networking and Learning Opportunities: Wander through gatherings of knowledge, where connections are forged and wisdom is shared. Engage in networking events, conferences, and workshops to meet potential partners and learn from their experiences.

Sustaining Relationships: Nurture the roots of your partnerships to ensure their enduring strength. Like a vibrant garden, relationships require ongoing care, communication, and trust-building. Regularly assess the effectiveness of the partnership, celebrate shared achievements, and acknowledge each partner's contributions.

Building Organizational Capacity

To ensure the long-term sustainability of your nonprofit organization, it is crucial to invest in building your organizational capacity. Capacity building involves developing the skills, systems, and infrastructure necessary to effectively deliver your programs, manage operations, and adapt to changing circumstances. Here are some strategies to consider:

Leadership Development: Invest in leadership development programs for your board members, staff, and volunteers. Provide opportunities for training, mentoring, and professional growth to enhance their skills and capabilities. It's also important to develop succession plans to ensure a smooth transition of leadership.

Staff Recruitment and Retention: Focus on hiring and retaining qualified and passionate staff members who align with your mission. Develop competitive compensation packages, offer growth opportunities, and foster a positive work culture that promotes employee satisfaction and engagement.

Volunteer Management: Create effective strategies for attracting, engaging, and retaining volunteers. Clearly define volunteer roles, provide training and support, and recognize their contributions. Foster a sense of community and ensure volunteers feel valued and connected to your organization's mission. For instance, a community kitchen might invite volunteers to monthly appreciation dinners where they hear updates on the program's impact and share feedback.

Technology and Systems: Invest in technology and systems that support your organization's operations and program delivery. This may include implementing donor management systems, financial software, project management tools, and communication platforms. Regularly assess and update your technology infrastructure to meet evolving program or security needs.

Financial Sustainability: Develop a diversified funding strategy to ensure financial sustainability once income streams are identified. Build reserves, consider establishing an endowment, and explore opportunities for revenue generation. Adopt sound financial management practices and engage in regular financial planning and budgeting processes.

Monitoring and Evaluation: Implement monitoring of organization wide systems to assess the effectiveness of your programming and planning in relation to your mission. Collect data, measure outcomes, and use the findings to inform decision-making and improve program effectiveness. Continuously learn from your experiences and adapt your strategies accordingly.

Continuous Learning and Improvement: Foster a culture of continuous learning and improvement within your organization. Encourage staff and volunteers to engage in professional development, attend trainings, and stay updated on best practices in your field. Regularly assess your programs, processes, and strategies to identify areas for improvement and innovation. Encourage personnel to engage with and further develop organizational wide education strategies.

Strategic Communications: Develop a strategic communications plan to effectively disseminate information regarding your organization's mission, impact, and value to key stakeholders. Utilize various communication channels, such as social media, website, newsletters, and media relations, to raise awareness, engage supporters, and build relationships with stakeholders.

Board Development: Invest in board development to ensure effective governance and strategic oversight. Continue to work toward recruiting board members with diverse backgrounds, skills, and networks, as board members are frequently elected or appointed over an organization's lifetime. Provide board training, orientation, and ongoing support to enhance their ability to fulfill their roles and responsibilities.

Collaboration and Knowledge Sharing: Encourage collaboration and knowledge sharing within your organization and with external stakeholders. Encourage staff and volunteers to share their expertise, lessons learned, and best practices. Seek partnerships with academic institutions and research organizations to leverage their expertise and resources. Engage in research partnerships (such as presentations, activities, or lectures) to contribute to the knowledge base in your field and enhance the evidence-based approach of your programs.

Financial Sustainability and Strategic Planning

Financial sustainability is a critical goal for nonprofit organizations to ensure their long-term viability and ability to fulfill their mission. Strategic financial planning plays a key role in achieving this sustainability. Here are some important points to understand about financial sustainability and strategic planning.

Diversification of Financing Sources: Relying on a single source of funding can pose risks to a nonprofit's financial sustainability. It is important to diversify financing sources by seeking support from multiple channels, such as grants, donations, fundraising events, earned income, partnerships, and collaborations. This can include local, state, national, and even international opportunities depending on your mission.

Long-Term Revenue Opportunities: Nonprofits should proactively explore and identify long-term revenue opportunities that align with their mission and values. This may include developing sustainable income-generating programs, fee-based services, social enterprise initiatives, or partnerships with businesses. By diversifying revenue streams, nonprofits can reduce reliance on unpredictable or restricted funding sources.

Accumulation of Financial Reserves: Building financial reserves is crucial for nonprofit organizations to weather unforeseen circumstances, manage cash flow fluctuations, and invest in future growth. Creating reserves can be achieved by setting aside a portion of surplus funds or through strategic planning for fundraising campaigns specifically aimed at building reserves. Accumulating reserves provides financial stability and enhances the organization's ability to respond to opportunities and challenges.

Thorough Sustainability Strategy: Nonprofits should develop a comprehensive sustainability strategy that addresses potential financial issues and outlines solutions for long-term development and stability. This strategy should consider factors such as revenue generation, expense management, risk assessment, and scenario planning. It should also incorporate measurable goals, timelines, and regular assessments to track progress and make necessary adjustments.

Engaging Stakeholders: Financial sustainability planning should involve key stakeholders, including board members, staff, donors, volunteers, and community members. Engage these stakeholders in the strategic planning process, seeking their input, insights, and support. This fosters a sense of collective responsibility and ownership in ensuring the financial sustainability of the organization.

Monitoring and Evaluation: Regularly monitor and evaluate the financial performance of the organization against its sustainability goals and strategic plans. Implement financial metrics and indicators to assess progress and make informed decisions. This allows for proactive management and timely adjustments to maintain financial health and sustainability.

By incorporating strategic financial planning into their operations, nonprofit organizations can enhance their financial sustainability, reduce risks, and ensure they have the resources to continue making a positive impact in their communities over the long term.

Taken together, these approaches to planning, funding, collaboration, and capacity building will position your nonprofit for long-term success. By focusing on big picture strategies, you can build the capacity of your nonprofit organization, strengthen its foundation, and increase its long-term sustainability over time. Remember that capacity building is an ongoing process that requires dedication and engagement from all managers and stakeholders. With strong organizational capacity, you'll be better equipped to navigate challenges, identify funding, maximize your impact, and achieve your mission.

CHAPTER 6:

EFFECTIVE PROGRAM MANAGEMENT AND IMPACT MEASUREMENT

Program Planning and Design

Program management is a critical aspect of achieving your nonprofit organization's mission and making a meaningful impact. By following a few steps, you can ensure that your programs are well-planned, efficiently implemented, and impactful.

Needs Assessment: Start by conducting a comprehensive needs assessment to identify the specific challenges or gaps your program aims to address. This assessment will provide a solid foundation for designing a program that is targeted and relevant. For example, a food security nonprofit might conduct surveys in a rural county to find that transportation is a bigger barrier to nutrition than food cost, leading them to create a mobile pantry program instead of a traditional food bank.

Goal Setting: Clearly define the goals and objectives of each major project or program. Make sure they are specific, measurable, attainable, relevant, and time-bound (SMART).

Align your program goals with your organization's mission and ensure they address the identified needs effectively. If your mission is to improve literacy rates, a SMART goal could be to increase third-grade reading proficiency in your county by 15% within three years through after-school tutoring.

Key Performance Indicators (KPIs): Once you have set your SMART goals, define KPIs to measure your progress toward achieving them. KPIs are specific, quantifiable metrics that indicate whether your program is on track and where adjustments may be needed. They should be relevant to your goals and actionable for decision-making. Keep the list focused, with just a few per program, to make tracking manageable. Examples include tracking the number of health screenings completed or improved attendance among youth participants. Review KPIs regularly, use the data to refine strategies, and share results with stakeholders to demonstrate progress.

Program Logic Model: Develop a program logic model that visually represents the inputs, activities, outputs, and outcomes of your program. This model will help you plan, implement, and evaluate your program effectively. It provides a clear representation of the theory of change underlying your program and allows personnel to interact with the model visually. For example, a youth mentorship program might map out resources (mentors, curriculum, meeting space), activities (weekly mentoring sessions), outputs (number of sessions delivered), and outcomes (improved school attendance). See the image included for a simplified chart you can use to try your first one.

PROGRAM LOGIC MODEL

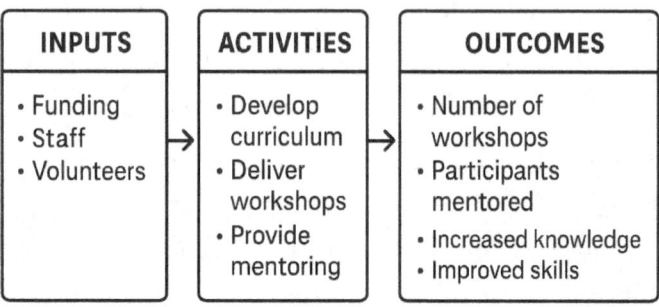

INPUTS	ACTIVITIES	OUTCOMES
• Funding • Staff • Volunteers	• Develop curriculum • Deliver workshops • Provide mentoring	• Number of workshops • Participants mentored • Increased knowledge • Improved skills

Program Components: Determine the key components and activities required to achieve the desired program outcomes. Identify the necessary resources, partnerships, and support needed to implement each component effectively. Develop a detailed implementation plan that outlines the timeline, responsible parties, and evaluation methods for each program component. This will help managers focus their time and attention.

Participant Engagement: Involve the target population meaningfully in the program design. Incorporate their insights and experiences to create programs that are more responsive to their needs and empower them as agents of change. Ensure their participation in decision-making, program design, and implementation processes. A homelessness services nonprofit, for example, might form a client advisory board so individuals with lived experience can help shape outreach efforts.

Collaboration and Partnerships: Seek opportunities for collaboration and partnerships to enhance program effectiveness. Identify organizations, community groups, and stake-holders that can contribute their expertise, resources, and networks to support your program. Establish clear roles, responsibilities, and communication channels to facilitate effective collaboration.

Budgeting and Resource Allocation: Develop a realistic budget that aligns with your program's goals and activities. Allocate resources effectively to ensure successful program implementation. Consider both financial resources and in-kind contributions, such as volunteer time or donated goods and services. Identify income and expenditures in order to chart anticipated cash flows. For example, when budgeting for a free health clinic, in-kind donations like medical supplies from a hospital partner might be valued alongside grant funding.

By following these steps, you can ensure that your nonprofit programs are well-designed, efficiently implemented, and impactful. Remember, effective program management is essential for achieving your mission and making a difference in the lives of those you serve.

Effective Program Implementation

Effective program implementation necessitates careful planning, efficient execution, and efficient resource management. Here are some extra tips to help you with program implementation:

Collaboration and Partnerships: Encourage collaboration and partnerships with other organizations, community groups, and stake-holders who may have aligned programming. Make use of their experience, skills, and networks to improve your program success. Working together allows you to pool resources, exchange information, and optimize the effect of your activities. Collaboration can lower program costs and alleviate personnel burdens. For example, two small animal rescue nonprofits might share transport vans and veterinary services to stretch their resources further.

Communication and Transparency: Establish open lines of contact with all stakeholders participating in the program. It is necessary to maintain transparency by disclosing program updates, triumphs, and difficulties. Effective communication encourages teamwork and ensures that everyone is informed and involved throughout the implementation process.

Continual Learning and Improvement: Create a culture of continual learning inside your organization. Encourage staff, volunteers, and program participants to reflect on their experiences, discuss lessons learned, and identify areas for improvement. Adopt a growth mentality and use feedback to generate program upgrades and innovation.

Community Engagement: Involve the local community in program conception and execution. Involve community people in decision-making, solicit their feedback, and enable them to participate actively in program activities. You can guarantee that your programs are relevant, responsive, and sustainable by incorporating the community. You can do this through participation in local events, lectures, or meetings within the community.

Sustainability Planning: Incorporate sustainability planning into program creation from the beginning. Consider your programs' long-term effect and scalability. Identify ways for securing continuous financing, building local expertise, and developing exit plans to ensure the program's viability beyond its initial implementation phase. These may be outgrowths of startup funding, or plans for new revenue services.

Cultural Sensitivity and Diversity: Recognize and appreciate the cultural variety of the populations you serve. Make certain that your program's execution takes cultural subtleties, values, and customs into consideration. Encourage inclusion and equitable access to program benefits for all persons, regardless of their origin or identity.

Ethical Considerations: Adhere to ethical norms in all stages of program execution. Protection of the rights and privacy of program participants is paramount. An organization has to maintain confidentiality, and emphasize the well-being and safety of all those engaged. Maintain integrity, openness, and accountability throughout the implementation process.

By implementing these recommendations into your program implementation strategy, you may increase its efficacy, encourage sustainability, and have a beneficial influence on the persons and communities you serve. Remember to constantly assess and change your methods to guarantee program success and maximize the benefits for all stakeholders.

Impact Measurement and Evaluation

Measuring and evaluating the impact of your programs is essential for demonstrating accountability, learning, and improving program effectiveness. Here are some additional points to consider to make impact measurement and evaluation more understandable and engaging:

Engage Stakeholders: Involve program participants, staff, and other stakeholders in the evaluation process. Seek their input on evaluation objectives, methods, and findings. Engaging stakeholders creates a sense of ownership and fosters a collaborative learning environment. For instance, a job training program could host a focus group of graduates to discuss which skills proved most valuable in their new jobs.

Use Visualizations: Utilize visual representations, such as charts, graphs, or infographics, to present evaluation findings. Visualizations can make complex data more accessible and engaging, allowing stakeholders to quickly grasp key insights and trends.

Share Lessons Learned: Highlight the lessons learned throughout the evaluation process with managers. Discuss both successes and challenges encountered and how they have informed program improvements. Sharing these lessons demonstrates a commitment to continuous learning and transparency.

Contextualize Findings: Provide context when reporting evaluation findings. Explain the program's operating environment, challenges faced, and other factors that may have influenced the outcomes. By contextualizing the findings, such as services offered or number of persons engaged in each program, you help stakeholders understand the broader context in which the program operates.

Use Plain Language: Present evaluation findings using plain and jargon-free language. Avoid technical terms or acronyms that may be unfamiliar to stakeholders. Using plain language ensures that the evaluation findings are easily understandable and accessible to a wide audience.

Celebrate Achievements: Acknowledge and celebrate the achievements and positive impact of your programs. Highlight success stories, testimonials, and personal anecdotes that demonstrate the tangible benefits experienced by program participants. Celebrating achievements not only inspires stakeholders but also reinforces the value and significance of your programs.

Utilize Technology: Leverage technology tools and platforms to streamline data collection, analysis, and reporting. Online surveys, data visualization software, and interactive dashboards can enhance the efficiency and accessibility of your evaluation process.

Foster a Learning Culture: Create a culture of learning within your organization by promoting a mindset of curiosity, reflection, and continuous improvement. Encourage staff and volunteers to engage in ongoing professional development, participate in evaluation discussions, and share insights and best practices.

By incorporating these additional factors into your impact, measurement, and evaluation practices, you can make the process more engaging, accessible, and valuable for stakeholders. Remember that effective evaluation is an iterative and dynamic process that drives learning, informs decision-making, and ultimately strengthens the impact of your programs.

Learning from Evaluation Findings

Effective program management involves utilizing evaluation findings to drive continuous improvement and inform decision-making. Here are some additional points to make the process more understandable and engaging.

Cultivate a Learning Culture: Foster a culture of learning and improvement within your organization. Encourage staff and volunteers to embrace evaluation findings as valuable insights for growth. Promote a mindset of curiosity, exploration, and innovation to drive ongoing learning and adaptation. For example, ask personnel to identify their understanding of the strengths and growth edges in the data.

Emphasize Actionable Recommendations: Ensure that evaluation findings include actionable recommendations. Provide practical guidance on how to address identified challenges and capitalize on strengths. Clear and specific recommendations make it easier for stakeholders to take concrete steps towards program improvement.

Share Success Stories: Highlight internal success stories, especially stories that demonstrate the positive outcomes achieved through program implementation. Use compelling narratives, visuals, and testimonials to effectively communicate the real-life impact of your programs. This storytelling approach can engage stakeholders emotionally and inspire further support.

Engage Program Participants: Involve program participants in the discussion and interpretation of evaluation findings. Their perspectives and insights are valuable in understanding the impact of your programs from their lived experiences. Create platforms for participants to share their feedback, suggestions, and ideas for program enhancement.

Use Data Visualization: Utilize data visualization techniques to present evaluation findings in a visually appealing and easily digestible format. Charts, graphs, and infographics can simplify complex information, making it more accessible and engaging for stakeholders who may not be familiar with technical terminology.

Experiment with Innovations: Encourage experimentation and innovation based on evaluation findings. Use the insights gained to explore new approaches, strategies, or interventions that could further enhance program outcomes. Be open to piloting new ideas and evaluating their effectiveness in a controlled and measured manner, based on your program data.

Collaborate with Peer Organizations: Collaborate with other nonprofit organizations and peers in the sector to share evaluation findings and exchange best practices. Jointly explore opportunities for learning, knowledge sharing, and collective problem-solving. Collaborative efforts can lead to greater collective impact and foster a culture of continuous improvement across the nonprofit sector.

Regular Evaluation Cycles: Establish a regular cycle for program evaluation to ensure that findings are continuously generated and utilized. Plan for periodic evaluations throughout the program's lifespan to track progress, identify emerging trends, and drive iterative improvements. Evaluation should be seen as an ongoing and iterative process rather than a one-time event.

By incorporating these aspects of evaluation, you can create a more engaging and impactful process for utilizing evaluation findings. Remember, the ultimate goal is to use evaluation as a catalyst for positive change, driving programmatic excellence and increasing the overall impact of your nonprofit organization.

CHAPTER 7:
FINANCIAL MANAGEMENT

Introduction to Financial Management

Financial management is critical to nonprofit organizations' success and sustainability. It includes a variety of tasks aimed at properly managing financial resources, such as budgeting, financial planning, monitoring, and reporting. Nonprofits may guarantee they have enough finances to meet their purpose, services, and operational needs by employing strong financial management procedures. In this chapter, we will look at the basic ideas and practices of nonprofit financial administration, giving you a thorough grasp of this critical component of organizational management.

Budgeting and Financial Planning

Budgeting and financial planning are fundamental components of effective financial management for nonprofit organizations. By following the below steps, you can begin to create a comprehensive budget and financial plan to guide your organization toward financial stability and success.

Revenue Forecasting: Estimate your expected revenue by considering various sources such as grants, donations, fundraising activities, and projected earned income. It's important to be realistic and conservative in your projections to avoid overestimating your income. Conduct thorough research and analysis to assess the potential revenue from each source. For example, if your animal rescue receives $40,000 from a grant, $25,000 from donors, $10,000 from an annual event, and $5,000 from adoption fees last year, you might project $80,000 for this year, but you might project $75,000 just to be safe in case it is a slow year.

Expense Projection: Identify and categorize your organization's expenses, including staff salaries, program costs, overhead expenses, marketing and communication expenses, and administrative costs. Prioritize expenses based on their significance to your mission and allocate resources accordingly. Review historical data and consult with relevant stakeholders to ensure accurate expense projections.

Expense Reimbursement: Clear procedures should be developed for reimbursing expenditures made by employees or volunteers on behalf of the organization. This involves defining the categories of costs that can be paid, the evidence necessary for reimbursement, and the approval procedure for reimbursement claims. With a well-defined procedure, you can guarantee that spending is valid, backed by sufficient paperwork, and in line with the organization's budget.

Program Budgeting: Develop individual program budgets that outline the costs associated with each program or project. This allows you to track and control expenses specific to each program, ensuring that resources are allocated effectively.

Ensure that your program budgets align with the overall organizational budget to maintain financial coherence.

Contingency Planning: Include a contingency fund in your budget to account for unforeseen expenses or emergencies. Having a financial buffer provides flexibility and helps mitigate potential risks. Set aside a portion of your budget as reserves to handle unexpected challenges without disrupting the overall financial stability of your organization.

Budget Monitoring and Review: Regularly monitor and review your budget to assess its accuracy and make necessary adjustments. Compare actual income and expenses to the budgeted amounts and analyze any variances. This will help you identify areas where you may need to reallocate resources, implement cost-saving measures, or revise your revenue generation strategies. Conduct budget reviews on a quarterly or semi-annual basis to ensure your financial plan remains aligned with your organization's goals.

Strategic Alignment: Align your budget and financial plan with your organization's strategic goals and priorities. Ensure that your financial resources are allocated in a way that supports your mission and maximizes your impact. Consider the short-term and long-term financial implications of your strategic decisions and prioritize investments that will contribute to your organization's growth and sustainability.

Stakeholder Engagement: Involve relevant stakeholders, such as board members, staff, and finance committee members, in the budgeting and financial planning process. Seek their input, expertise, and buy-in to ensure that the budget reflects the collective goals and priorities of your organization. Regularly communicate and report on financial matters to keep stakeholders informed and engaged.

Flexibility and Adaptability: Recognize that budgets are not set in stone and may need to be adjusted as circumstances change. Be prepared to adapt your financial plan based on emerging opportunities, challenges, or shifts in funding sources. Maintain flexibility in your budgeting process to accommodate unforeseen changes and seize new opportunities that align with your organization's mission.

Management of Cashflow

Effective cash flow management is critical for nonprofit organizations in order to continue operations and satisfy financial obligations. Here are some strategies that NGOs may use to manage cash flow more effectively:

Cash Flow Forecasting: Nonprofits should create a cash flow projection, which entails projecting the time and quantities of projected financial inflows and outflows. This projection aids in forecasting periods of monetary surplus or shortage. It considers revenue from different sources, such as grants, gifts, fundraising efforts, and earned income, as well as predicted costs. For example, a youth center knows a $20,000 grant arrives in January, but rent and payroll are due every month. Their cash flow chart shows they'll run short after July, so they schedule a summer fundraiser to fill the gap. These forecasts balance these against the timeline of expenditures to assure that the nonprofit remains cash positive across the entire fiscal period. Nonprofits may make educated judgments and take appropriate steps to efficiently manage their cash flow if they have a clear picture of their predicted financial situation.

Receivables and Payables: Nonprofits should keep a tight eye on their receivables and payables. Receivables are monies owing to the organization, such as unpaid grant payments, outstanding direct revenue invoices, or donations. To ensure timely receipt of payments, nonprofits should follow up on receivables and create effective collection practices. Payables, on the other hand, are monies due by the business to suppliers, vendors, or service providers. Payment of payables on time is critical for maintaining good relationships and avoiding supply chain interruptions.

Strategic Financial Decision-Making: Nonprofits should make strategic financial decisions that coincide with their long-term goals and objectives. This involves allocating spending based on the organization's objective, effect, and financial sustainability. Nonprofits may optimize their cash flow and distribute resources more efficiently by making educated decisions regarding investments, program expansions, or cost-cutting initiatives.

Collaboration and Communication: Nonprofits should encourage collaboration and communication among employees, board members, and stakeholders when it comes to cash flow management. It is critical to foster a culture of financial accountability and openness. Regular meetings and conversations regarding cash flow, financial performance, and resource allocation allow stakeholders to contribute feedback, discover opportunities, and work together to ensure a healthy cash flow.

Financial Reporting and Transparency

Financial reporting and transparency are crucial elements for nonprofit organizations to build trust and maintain strong relationships with stakeholders. Many steps can be taken to enhance financial reporting and transparency.

Making Regular Financial Reports: Nonprofit organizations are frequently expected to produce regular financial reports to stakeholders such as board members, funders, and regulatory agencies. Financial reporting entails creating accurate and complete accounts that describe the financial operations of the business, such as income, spending, assets, and liabilities. These reports allow stakeholders to examine the financial health of the organization, make educated decisions, and ensure openness and accountability.

Annual Reports: Publish an annual report that goes beyond the numbers and provides a comprehensive overview of your organization's achievements, impact, and financial performance. Include narratives, success stories, and testimonials that illustrate the real-world outcomes of your programs. In addition to financial data, highlight the social and environmental impact created by your organization. For instance, a literacy nonprofit might show that 85% of its budget went to tutoring programs and share a short success story about a student who improved two reading levels in one year.

Donor Communication: Foster open and transparent communication with donors and funders. Regularly update them on the progress and impact of your programs, as well as how their contributions are being utilized. Provide specific examples and stories that demonstrate the difference their support is making. Be responsive to donor inquiries and requests for additional information.

Compliance with Legal and Regulatory Obligations: Nonprofit organizations are subject to a variety of legal and regulatory financial management obligations. Filing tax returns, conforming to accounting standards, abiding to fundraising restrictions, and submitting financial information to government authorities or oversight organizations are examples of these. To protect the organization's legal position and reputation, it is critical to be updated about applicable rules and regulations and to assure compliance.

Independent Financial Audits: Conduct periodic external audits by external auditors to validate your financial statements and demonstrate your commitment to transparency and accountability. The audit findings provide an objective assessment of your organization's financial health and adherence to accounting standards. Share the audit reports with stakeholders to reinforce trust and credibility.

Donor Restrictions and Reporting: Respect and honor donor restrictions on the use of funds. Maintain accurate records and provide regular reports to donors on how their restricted funds are being utilized. Clearly communicate the impact achieved through their contributions and demonstrate the alignment of outcomes with the donors' intentions.

Online Transparency: Leverage digital platforms to enhance transparency. Make financial information easily accessible on your organization's website, including annual reports, audited financial statements, and IRS Form 990. Consider using interactive tools and visualizations to present financial data in a user-friendly and engaging manner.

Whistleblower Policy: Implement a whistleblower policy that encourages staff and stakeholders to report any suspected financial misconduct or irregularities. Provide a safe and confidential mechanism for reporting, investigate reported concerns promptly, and take appropriate action if any wrong-doing is identified.

Stakeholder Engagement: Actively engage with stakeholders by soliciting their input and feedback on financial matters. Organize forums, meetings, or advisory groups where stakeholders can provide insights and suggestions. Incorporate their perspectives into decision-making processes, particularly those related to financial management and resource allocation.

Internal Controls and Risk Management

Internal controls and risk management are essential components of financial management for nonprofit organizations. They help safeguard assets, prevent fraud, and ensure compliance with rules and regulations. Below are some key points to understand and consider.

Segregation of Roles: Separate financial responsibilities among different individuals to create checks and balances. For example, the person who authorizes transactions should not be the same person who records them. This segregation of roles helps prevent errors or fraudulent activities by requiring multiple individuals to be involved in financial processes.

Regular Reconciliations: Perform regular reconciliations of financial accounts, such as bank statements, to ensure that the recorded transactions match the actual transactions. This helps identify discrepancies or errors promptly, allowing for timely corrections and ensuring the accuracy of financial records.

Documentation and Record-Keeping: Maintain comprehensive and organized financial documentation and records. This includes invoices, receipts, bank statements, and other supporting documents. Accurate and complete documentation enables transparency, facilitates audits, and provides evidence of financial transactions and compliance.

Fraud Prevention and Detection: Implement measures to prevent and detect fraudulent activities. This can include implementing strict approval processes for financial transactions, conducting background checks on employees handling finances, and promoting a culture of ethics and integrity within the organization. Encourage staff to report any suspicious activities and establish a confidential reporting mechanism.

Risk Assessment and Management: Conduct regular risk assessments to identify potential financial risks and develop strategies to manage them effectively. This includes analyzing external risks, such as changes in funding or regulatory environment, as well as internal risks, such as inadequate controls or reliance on a single source of funding. Develop risk mitigation plans and monitor their effectiveness. A food pantry, for example, might see that one donor supplies 60% of its food and decide to reduce risk by adding new suppliers and building a three-month reserve of staple items.

Training and Staff Development: Provide opportunities for training and ongoing development opportunities to staff involved in financial management. This ensures that they have the necessary knowledge and skills to perform their roles effectively and adhere to financial policies and procedures. Regularly communicate updates and changes in financial regulations or internal processes to staff.

Continuous Improvement: Continuously review and improve your procedures based on lessons learned, feedback, and evolving best practices. Regularly assess the effectiveness of existing controls and make adjustments as needed to address emerging risks or operational changes.

Board Oversight: Engage the board of directors in overseeing internal controls and risk management. The board should review and approve financial policies, receive regular reports on internal controls and risk assessments, and provide guidance and oversight to ensure the organization's financial stability and compliance.

Strong financial management is the foundation of a nonprofit's ability to fulfill its mission and adapt to changing circumstances. By combining thoughtful budgeting, careful cash flow oversight, transparent reporting, and robust internal controls, organizations can safeguard their resources and inspire stakeholder confidence. The principles outlined in this chapter not only protect against risk but also position nonprofits to grow, innovate, and maximize their impact. Ultimately, a disciplined and transparent approach to finances empowers an organization to serve its community with consistency and credibility.

CHAPTER 8:

GOVERNANCE AND BOARD DEVELOPMENT

Introduction to Governance

A successful and sustained nonprofit organization is built on strong governance. It serves as the foundation for making strategic choices, assuring accountability, and steering the business toward its objective. This chapter digs into the fundamental ideas and practices of governance and board building, enabling organizations to build strong and successful governance structures. Nonprofits may increase their openness, trustworthiness, and overall organizational success by following strong governance procedures.

Organizations encounter complicated problems and growing stakeholder expectations in the nonprofit sector's ever-changing context. Effective governance provides a road map for managing these hurdles and capitalizing on possibilities for development and impact. It entails creating defined duties and responsibilities, cultivating a culture of responsibility and honesty, and encouraging active engagement of board members and stakeholders.

Mission-Driven Leadership: Governance should be based on the organization's mission and values. Board members should embody and advocate the mission, ensuring that all choices are in line with the organization's purpose and benefit the communities it serves.

Board Composition and Recruitment: Having a diversified and knowledgeable board is essential for good governance. The board should be made up of people with diverse experiences, backgrounds, and opinions that represent the organization's goal and the communities it serves. Thoughtful recruiting methods and continuing board development ensure that the board has the essential skills and knowledge to govern the company. For example, a health-focused nonprofit might recruit a mix of board members including a local physician, a marketing professional, a community advocate, and a financial expert to cover both mission knowledge and operational skills.

Clear duties and obligations: Effective governance requires clearly outlining the duties and obligations of board members, officials, and committees. Setting attendance, active involvement, and fiduciary responsibility requirements is part of this. Board members should have a thorough awareness of their responsibilities and the governance framework.

Strategic Planning and Oversight: The board is responsible for strategic planning and overseeing organizational operations. Board members should actively engage in determining the strategic direction of the business, monitoring progress, and evaluating performance against goals. Regular examination and change of strategic plans ensures agility and responsiveness to the organization's and its stakeholders' changing demands. For instance, if a youth mentorship nonprofit sees demand growing faster than expected, the board might revise the strategic plan mid-year to add a new part-time program coordinator and expand mentor recruitment goals.

Financial Stewardship and Accountability: The board is accountable for the organization's financial health. This involves budgeting, financial reporting, and ensuring compliance with financial rules. Board members should demonstrate fiscal responsibility, implement internal controls, and encourage financial openness.

Effective Communication: Effective governance requires more than well-structured and productive board meetings. Board members should be provided with timely and appropriate information prior to meetings in order to make informed decisions. They should also be encouraged to ask questions and contribute whenever appropriate to the organization's managers.

Board Development and Succession Planning: Continuous board development and succession planning guarantee that good governance is sustained. Providing board members with continual education and training opportunities improves their skills and expertise. Succession planning ensures that leadership transitions smoothly and that governance procedures remain consistent.

Ethical and Legal Compliance: Nonprofit organizations must adhere to high ethical standards as well as legal and regulatory regulations. To preserve integrity and accountability, the board should adopt and implement a code of ethics, conflict of interest regulations, and other governance-related policies.

Nonprofits may develop a robust governance foundation by embracing these concepts and practices, allowing them to manage problems, capture opportunities, and successfully achieve their goals. Effective governance enables them to create a long-term effect, gain stakeholder confidence, and ensure long-term viability.

Board Roles and Responsibilities

The board of directors serves as the backbone of governance for nonprofit organizations, providing leadership, oversight, and strategic direction. Understanding and fulfilling their roles and responsibilities is essential for effective decision-making and organizational success. This section explores the key roles and responsibilities that boards undertake to ensure strong governance and impactful outcomes.

Mission and Strategic Direction: The board takes charge of defining and communicating the organization's mission and vision. They guide the development of a strategic direction that aligns with the mission and establishes goals for the organization's growth and impact. By keeping the mission at the forefront, the board ensures that all activities contribute to the organization's overarching purpose.

Governance Oversight: Upholding legal and regulatory compliance is a primary responsibility of the board. They establish governance policies and procedures to ensure transparency, accountability, and ethical behavior. The board also oversees financial management, risk assessment, and the implementation of mechanisms to ensure the organization operates within legal boundaries.

Board Meetings and Decision-Making: Regular board meetings serve as platforms for discussions, decision-making, and collaboration. Board members actively engage in these meetings, bringing their expertise and perspectives to the table. They come prepared, ask critical questions, and collectively make informed decisions that guide the organization's activities. Records of these meetings are kept to track major decisions and monitor goal oriented steps in the long term.

Fiduciary Responsibilities: The board bears fiduciary responsibilities to safeguard the organization's assets and resources. They oversee financial management, approving budgets, monitoring financial performance, and ensuring responsible and effective resource utilization. By exercising sound financial stewardship, the board secures the organization's sustainability.

Fundraising and Resource Development: Board members play an instrumental role in fundraising and resource development efforts. They leverage their networks and connections to cultivate relationships with donors, advocate for the organization's mission, and contribute to fundraising strategies. A museum board member, for example, might introduce the director to a corporate contact, resulting in a new exhibit sponsorship. By actively participating in resource mobilization, the board helps secure the necessary funds to advance the organization's goals.

Board-CEO Relationship: Establishing a strong and collaborative relationship with the CEO or executive director is vital for effective leadership. The board provides guidance, support, and oversight to the CEO, ensuring alignment with the organization's strategic direction and evaluating their performance. This relationship fosters a shared vision and effective management.

By embracing these roles and responsibilities, nonprofit boards contribute to strong governance, enhance organizational credibility, and drive meaningful change. Their leadership and commitment are vital in guiding nonprofits toward achieving their missions and making a difference in the communities they serve.

Board Governance Practices

To ensure effective governance, nonprofit organizations should adopt best practices that enhance board performance and effectiveness. By implementing the following practices, nonprofits can optimize their board's leadership, decision-making, and overall impact:

Board Orientation and Training: Provide new board members with comprehensive orientation to familiarize them with their roles, responsibilities, and the organization's mission. Offer ongoing training opportunities to enhance their knowledge and skills in areas such as governance, finance, fundraising, and strategic planning.

Board Committees: On larger boards, establish board committees focused on specific areas of governance, such as finance, fundraising, governance, and program oversight. Assign board members to committees based on their skills and interests. These committees facilitate in-depth discussions, analysis, and decision-making on specific issues, ensuring thorough and focused attention.

Board Evaluations: Conduct regular board evaluations to assess the board's performance, effectiveness, and adherence to governance principles. Utilize evaluation results to identify areas for improvement and implement strategies to enhance board effectiveness. This process promotes self-reflection, continuous improvement, and accountability.

Board Engagement and Accountability: Foster a culture of active engagement and accountability among board members.

Encourage open and constructive dialogue, promote transparency in decision-making processes, and hold board members accountable for their commitments and responsibilities. This culture strengthens board dynamics and ensures collective responsibility.

Board-Staff Collaboration: Cultivate strong collaboration between the board and staff members. Foster open communication, mutual respect, and a shared understanding of roles and responsibilities. Ensure that the board provides support and guidance while respecting the executive leadership of the staff. This collaboration harnesses the strengths of both groups for organizational success.

Continual Learning and Adaptation: Encourage a culture of continual learning and adaptation within the board. Stay informed about emerging trends, best practices, and changes in the nonprofit sector. Adapt governance practices as needed to respond to the evolving needs and challenges of the organization. This adaptability ensures the board remains relevant and effective.

By implementing these best practices, nonprofit organizations can strengthen their governance structures, empower their boards, and maximize their impact in achieving their missions. Effective governance sets the stage for organizational success, accountability, and the fulfillment of their important social and community objectives.

Board Development and Succession Planning

Maintaining a strong and capable board over time is essential for the success and sustainability of nonprofit organizations. To achieve this, organizations should look at board development and succession planning with focus on a number of important elements.

Board Self-Assessment: Conduct regular board self-assessments to evaluate the board's composition, performance, and effectiveness. This assessment helps identify strengths, weaknesses, and areas for improvement. Use the results to develop strategies for enhancing board performance.

Leadership Development: Provide opportunities for board members to enhance their leadership skills and knowledge. Offer training, workshops, and mentorship programs that focus on board governance, strategic planning, fundraising, and other relevant areas. These initiatives empower board members to fulfill their roles effectively.

Succession Planning: Develop a succession plan to ensure smooth transitions when board members' terms expire or leadership positions need to be filled. Identify potential candidates who possess the necessary skills and qualifications. Provide training and mentorship to prepare them for future board roles.

Engaging Former Board Members: Maintain relationships with former board members who have made significant contributions to the organization. Seek their input, advice, and support as appropriate. Consider establishing an honorary board or advisory council to involve former members in a meaningful capacity.

Board Knowledge Management: Establish systems to capture and preserve institutional knowledge within the board. Maintain comprehensive records of board meetings, minutes, and key documents. This ensures continuity and facilitates smooth transitions by providing access to historical information.

Board Governance Training: Offer ongoing training and professional development opportunities for board members on governance practices, legal and ethical responsibilities, and emerging trends in the nonprofit sector. Equip board members with the necessary knowledge and skills to excel in their roles.

Board-CEO Succession Planning: Develop a succession plan for the CEO or executive director position to ensure continuity of leadership. Identify potential successors, provide mentorship and development opportunities, and establish a clear process for selecting the next CEO when necessary.

By implementing these steps, nonprofit organizations can foster board development, strengthen governance practices, and ensure smooth leadership transitions. An effective board drives organizational success, ensures accountability, and advances the organization's mission for the benefit of the communities they serve.

Ethical Considerations in Governance

Ethics and integrity are vital elements of effective governance in nonprofit organizations. Upholding ethical standards, practicing transparency, and being accountable are essential for maintaining public trust and safeguarding the organization's reputation. There are key ethical considerations in nonprofit governance that serve to uphold ethical standards.

Conflict of Interest: Establish clear policies and procedures to prevent conflicts of interest among board members and staff. Disclose potential conflicts and take appropriate measures to mitigate them. For example, if a board member owns a catering company being considered for an event contract, they should disclose the relationship and recuse themselves from the decision. We want board members to make decisions in the best interest of the organization, avoiding personal gain or favoritism.

Transparency and Accountability: Practice transparency in all aspects of the organization's operations. Provide stakeholders and the public with access to information such as financial statements, impact reports, and governance policies. Communicate openly about decision-making processes, ensuring alignment with the organization's mission and values.

Responsible Stewardship of Resources: Ensure responsible and ethical management of the organization's resources, including finances, human resources, and assets. Use funds and assets in ways that maximize the organization's mission impact and avoid wastefulness or misuse.

Confidentiality and Data Privacy: Safeguard confidential information and respect the privacy rights of individuals associated with the organization, such as donors, staff, volunteers, and beneficiaries. Establish protocols for handling and protecting sensitive data against unauthorized access or disclosure.

Whistleblower Protection: Establish a mechanism for reporting potential wrongdoing or unethical behavior within the organization. Provide a safe and confidential process for whistleblowers to come forward and protect them from retaliation. Take appropriate action to address reported concerns or violations.

Diversity, Equity, and Inclusion: Promote diversity, equity, and inclusion within the organization's governance processes. Ensure the board reflects the communities served and actively fosters an inclusive and equitable environment for all stakeholders. Make decisions that consider diverse needs and perspectives.

Compliance with Laws and Regulations: Stay informed about applicable laws, regulations, and best practices related to nonprofit governance. Comply with all legal and regulatory requirements, including tax and reporting obligations. Seek legal advice when needed to ensure compliance.

Ethical Fundraising: Adhere to ethical fundraising practices, including honesty and accuracy in communications, respect for donor intent, and responsible use of funds. Avoid misleading or coercive tactics and ensure donations align with donors' intentions.

Responsible Advocacy: If engaged in advocacy or lobbying, conduct these activities ethically and in compliance with laws. Maintain transparency in advocacy efforts and clearly differentiate between lobbying and programmatic work.

Continuous Improvement: Regularly evaluate and review governance practices to identify areas for improvement and ensure ongoing adherence to ethical standards. Seek feedback from stakeholders to inform decision-making and governance processes.

By upholding ethical principles, nonprofit organizations demonstrate their commitment to integrity, accountability, and responsible management. Ethical governance builds trust among stakeholders, strengthens the organization's reputation, and enables nonprofits to effectively fulfill their missions and create a positive change in their communities.

CHAPTER 9:

EVALUATION AND IMPACT ASSESSMENT

Introduction to Evaluation and Impact Assessment

Evaluation and impact assessment are critical activities that allow nonprofit organizations to analyze the performance of their programs and efforts. These procedures assist nonprofits in gaining insights about the consequences and accomplishments of their work, understanding what works and what does not, and making educated decisions to increase their effect.

In this chapter, we will look at essential ideas and methodologies for conducting evaluations and quantifying effects in the nonprofit sector. Nonprofit organizations may obtain accurate data, examine the efficacy of their programs, and demonstrate their worth to stakeholders and funders by adopting these principles and employing effective evaluation methodologies. We will discuss aspects of logic models, result mapping, surveys, interviews, data analysis, and others.

Evaluation and impact assessments offer vital information about the outcomes and changes that nonprofits are achieving. They assist organizations in understanding how effectively they are accomplishing their purpose, identify areas for development, and make evidence-based decisions to optimize their performance.

Nonprofits may successfully communicate their outcomes and successes to donors, funders, and the wider society after assessing impact. Demonstrating the value of their work boosts credibility, deepens connections with stakeholders, and raises support for their goal.

Nonprofit organizations may obtain a better knowledge of the success of their work and make educated decisions to achieve positive change by adopting evaluation and impact assessment procedures. This helps them to constantly improve their programs, better their services, and have a stronger influence in the communities they serve.

Let us now look at the essential ideas and methodologies for conducting evaluations and assessing effect in nonprofit organizations, with the goal of empowering them to better understand, share, and magnify their results and successes.

Importance of Evaluation and Impact Assessment

Evaluation and impact assessment play a crucial role in helping nonprofit organizations understand the effectiveness and impact of their programs. By utilizing these processes, organizations can gain valuable insights that inform decision-making, improve program outcomes, and demonstrate accountability to stakeholders.

Understand Outcomes: Evaluation allows organizations to assess whether their programs are achieving the intended outcomes and goals in the community. By collecting and analyzing data on community program outcomes, organizations can identify areas of success and areas that may require improvement or adjustments. For instance, a literacy nonprofit might measure whether students' reading levels improve by at least one grade over the course of a year. This understanding helps shape future program efforts and ensures that resources are directed towards activities that yield meaningful results.

Improve Program Design: Evaluation results provide valuable information that informs program design and implementation. By analyzing the data collected during the evaluation process, organizations can identify strengths and weaknesses, determine what strategies are effective, and make evidence-based decisions to refine their programs. This iterative process of improvement optimizes the use of resources and maximizes program effectiveness.

Demonstrate Accountability: Evaluation provides tangible evidence of an organization's accountability to its stakeholders. By conducting evaluations and sharing the findings, nonprofits can demonstrate the responsible use of resources and their commitment to achieving meaningful outcomes. A food bank might show that 95% of its funding goes directly toward meal distribution, supported by data from an independent audit. This transparency builds trust and credibility with funders, beneficiaries, and the broader community.

Inform Strategic Planning: Evaluation findings guide strategic planning and resource allocation. By examining the impact of programs and initiatives, organizations can identify priorities, set realistic goals, and align their activities with their mission and vision. Evaluation data provides valuable insights into which strategies are most effective, enabling organizations to make informed decisions about future directions and resource allocation.

Enhance Learning and Knowledge Sharing: Evaluation fosters a culture of learning and knowledge sharing within organizations. Through the evaluation process, nonprofits can identify best practices, lessons learned, and areas for improvement. By sharing this knowledge internally and externally, organizations contribute to the sector's collective understanding and promote continuous improvement in program delivery.

By embracing evaluation and impact assessment, nonprofit organizations can gain a deeper understanding of their programs' effectiveness, improve outcomes, and demonstrate accountability. These practices foster a culture of learning, inform decision-making, and enable organizations to make a more significant and sustainable impact in the communities they serve.

Evaluation Planning

Effective evaluation begins with a well-designed evaluation plan. By following key steps, nonprofit organizations can ensure that their evaluation efforts are focused, comprehensive, and yield reliable and actionable insights.

Define Evaluation Questions: Start by clearly articulating the evaluation questions you want to answer. These questions should directly align with your organization's goals and objectives. They should focus on assessing the outcomes and impact of your programs. A community health program might ask, "Has the vaccination rate among children under five increased since the start of our outreach campaign?" By defining the evaluation questions upfront, you establish a clear direction for your evaluation efforts.

Identify Evaluation Methods: Determine the most appropriate methods for gathering data to answer your evaluation questions. This may involve using surveys, interviews, focus groups, observations, case studies, or a combination of methods. Consider the resources, timeframe, and expertise needed for each method, and select the ones that best align with your evaluation goals and available resources.

Develop an Evaluation Framework: Create an evaluation framework that outlines the key elements of your evaluation. This framework should include the evaluation questions, the chosen data collection methods, data analysis techniques, and reporting requirements. By developing a framework, you establish a structured and systematic approach to guide the remainder of your evaluation process.

Establish Data Collection Tools: Develop data collection tools that are aligned with your evaluation questions and methods. These tools may include surveys, interview guides, or observation protocols. It's important to pilot test these tools to ensure their effectiveness, relevance, and clarity. Pilot testing allows you to identify any necessary adjustments or improvements before implementing them in the actual evaluation.

Determine Sampling and Data Collection Procedures: Determine the appropriate sample size and sampling methods for data collection. Identify the target population or sample group that will provide the necessary information to answer your evaluation questions. Additionally, establish procedures for data collection, ensuring that ethical considerations and informed consent are upheld throughout the process.

By following these steps, nonprofit organizations can design an evaluation plan that is tailored to their specific needs and objectives. A well-designed evaluation plan provides a roadmap for collecting and analyzing data effectively, ensuring that the evaluation process is rigorous, informative, and ultimately supports informed decision-making and program improvement.

Data Collection and Analysis

Once the evaluation plan is in place, it's time to proceed with data collection and analysis. There are practices that can assist in ensuring a robust and informative evaluation process.

Collect Data: Implement the data collection methods outlined in your evaluation plan. Collect data from relevant sources, such as program participants, staff members, stakeholders, or external partners. Ensure data quality by adhering to proper documentation practices, validating data for accuracy and completeness, and implementing quality control measures to minimize errors.

Analyze Data: Use appropriate data analysis techniques to examine and make sense of the collected data. Depending on the nature of your evaluation, this may involve quantitative analysis, qualitative analysis, or a mixed-methods approach. Analyze the data based on your evaluation questions and objectives, identifying patterns, trends, and themes that emerge from the data. Feel free to seek external support to analyze your data if it is more voluminous or complex than can be handled in-house.

Interpret Findings: Interpret the evaluation findings within the context of your evaluation questions and program goals. Identify key insights, strengths, weaknesses, and areas for improvement. Consider any contextual factors that may have influenced the findings and draw meaningful conclusions from the analyzed data. Look for patterns or connections that provide a deeper understanding of your program's impact.

Communicate Results: Prepare a comprehensive evaluation report that effectively communicates the findings, conclusions, and recommendations of your evaluation. Present the data in a clear, concise, and accessible manner, using visual aids such as graphs, charts, or infographics to enhance the presentation. Tailor the report to different audiences, ensuring that the information is relevant and understandable to various stake-holders, including program staff, funders, and beneficiaries.

Utilize Feedback Loops: Create feedback loops within your organization to ensure that evaluation findings are shared and acted upon. Engage program staff, board members, and other relevant stakeholders in discussions about the evaluation results. Encourage open dialogue and collaborative problem-solving to address any identified areas for improvement and maximize the impact of your evaluation efforts.

By following these practices, nonprofit organizations can effectively collect, analyze, interpret, and communicate evaluation findings, leading to informed decision-making, program improvement, and enhanced accountability to stakeholders.

Measuring Impact

When measuring impact, it's important to go beyond program outputs and focus on understanding the broader outcomes and long-term changes resulting from your organization's work. There are a number of approaches to consider.

Outcome Measurement: Adopt outcome measurement approaches that focus on capturing the specific changes or outcomes directly influenced by your organization's activities.

Develop a theory of change or visual logic model that outlines the causal pathways from inputs to outcomes. Identify relevant indicators to measure these outcomes and track progress over time.

Impact Evaluation: Implement impact evaluation methodologies to assess the overall impact of your programs. This involves comparing the outcomes achieved by program participants with a suitable comparison group or baseline data. Impact evaluations provide insights into the extent to which your programs are producing the desired changes in the target population.

Qualitative Methods: Incorporate qualitative methods, such as interviews, focus groups, and case studies, to gather rich and in-depth information about the impact of your programs. These methods can capture nuanced changes, personal experiences, and stories of transformation that numerical metrics alone may not fully capture. A participant in a job training program might describe how gaining employment improved their family's stability, a nuance not shown in numbers alone.

Data Triangulation: Utilize a combination of quantitative and qualitative data sources to triangulate findings and enhance the credibility of your impact assessment. By analyzing multiple sources of data, including surveys, interviews, and program data, you can gain a more comprehensive understanding of the impact achieved.

Longitudinal Studies: Consider conducting longitudinal studies to track changes and outcomes over an extended period. Longitudinal studies allow you to assess the sustainability of program impact and understand how changes unfold and evolve over time.

Benchmarking and Comparative Analysis: Benchmark your organization's impact against industry standards, best practices, or similar programs. Engage in comparative analysis to understand how your organization's outcomes and impact compare to others in the field. This can provide valuable insights for program improvement and strategic decision-making.

Feedback and Continuous Learning: Foster a culture of feedback and continuous learning within your organization. Regularly solicit feedback from program participants, beneficiaries, and other stakeholders to understand their perspectives on the impact of your programs. Use this feedback to inform program adjustments and improvements.

By adopting these approaches, nonprofit organizations can gain a deeper understanding of their impact, enhance accountability, and make informed decisions to maximize their positive social and environmental outcomes.

Learning and Continuous Improvement

Evaluation and impact assessment should be viewed as ongoing learning processes that allow nonprofit organizations to continuously improve their programs and make a greater impact. Specific ways to facilitate this can be built into your mission or procedures.

Cultivating a Learning Culture: Foster a culture within the organization that values learning, evaluation, and continuous improvement. Encourage staff members to embrace a growth mindset and view evaluations as opportunities for learning rather than as judgments.

Engaging Stakeholders: Involve stakeholders, including program participants, staff members, board members, and external partners, in the evaluation and impact assessment process. Seek their input, perspectives, and experiences to gain a holistic understanding of program outcomes and to identify areas for improvement.

Adapting and Iterating: Use evaluation findings to inform program adaptations and iterations. Apply the lessons learned from evaluations to refine program strategies, modify approaches, and resolve weaknesses or gaps. Embrace a culture of experimentation and flexibility to continuously refine program implementation.

Building Evaluation Capacity: Invest in building the organization's evaluation capacity. Provide training and resources to staff members involved in evaluation and impact assessment. Develop internal expertise to conduct evaluations, analyze data, and draw meaningful conclusions.

Incorporating Monitoring and Evaluation Systems: Implement robust monitoring and evaluation systems that allow for regular tracking of program activities, outputs, and outcomes. Monitor program performance against targets and use the data collected to inform ongoing decision-making and program adjustments.

Learning from Others: Engage with peers, professional networks, and the broader nonprofit community to learn from their experiences and best practices in evaluation and impact assessment. Participate in conferences, workshops, and knowledge-sharing platforms to stay informed about emerging trends and innovative approaches.

Allocating Resources: Allocate resources, including time and funding, to support evaluation and impact assessment activities. Recognize that evaluation is an investment in the organization's learning and improvement process.

By embracing a culture of learning and continuous improvement, nonprofit organizations can drive positive change, enhance program effectiveness, and achieve their missions more effectively.

CHAPTER 10

ETHICAL CONSIDERATIONS IN NONPROFIT ORGANIZATIONS

Introduction to Ethical Considerations

Nonprofit organizations' operations, decision-making, and relationships with stakeholders are all guided by ethics. This chapter discusses the significance of ethical issues for nonprofit executives, staff members, and volunteers. Organizations may build trust, retain credibility, and maintain their integrity by knowing and adhering to ethical standards.

Ethics provides a moral compass that guides the behavior and activities of persons inside nonprofit organizations. They include a variety of ideas and values like as honesty, openness, justice, responsibility, and respect for the rights and dignity of others. Adherence to these principles ensures that organizations perform ethically and meet their social duties.

Nonprofit executives are critical in establishing the ethical tone and fostering an organizational culture of integrity. They must set a good example by displaying ethical conduct and making ethical judgments that are consistent with the goal and values of the company. By emphasizing ethics, leaders develop trust and create an environment in which staff and volunteers are driven to perform ethically in their responsibilities.

Staff and volunteers are also responsible for upholding ethical standards. They must follow ethical rules and codes of behavior while preserving professional integrity in relationships with coworkers, beneficiaries, donors, and the larger community. Their ethical behavior helps the organization's reputation and capacity to carry out its goal efficiently.

Furthermore, ethical concerns extend beyond internal operations to include external interactions. Nonprofits must maintain open and transparent communication with its stakeholders, who include donors, funders, partners, and the communities they serve. They must guarantee that resources are handled appropriately, that conflicts of interest are avoided, and that donor intent is honored. Ethical methods establish long-term partnerships by fostering trust and attracting support.

Exploring the ethical concerns that drive nonprofit operations may help leaders, staff members, and volunteers overcome complicated challenges, make moral judgments, and defend their organizations' ideals and integrity. Adopting ethics as a guiding framework increases the nonprofit sector's potential to effect good change and make a significant contribution to society.

Ethical Leadership

Nonprofit leaders play a crucial role in setting the ethical tone and fostering a culture of integrity within their organizations. Using key practices for ethical leadership allows organizations to maintain integrity and fly in this area.

Lead by Example: Leaders should embody the ethical principles they expect from others. By consistently demonstrating ethical behavior, such as honesty, integrity, and transparency, leaders establish a foundation of trust and inspire others to act ethically. For example, a director of a housing nonprofit might refuse a lucrative donation from a developer whose projects have displaced vulnerable residents, reinforcing the organization's values in action.

Foster Ethical Culture: Leaders should create an organizational culture that values ethics and encourages open communication. They can promote discussions on ethical issues, provide guidance on ethical decision-making, and establish channels for reporting ethical concerns. Developing and communicating a code of ethics or conduct helps clarify expected standards of behavior.

Establish Accountability: Leaders should establish mechanisms for accountability and hold individuals responsible for their actions and decisions. Clearly communicating expectations regarding ethical conduct and implementing systems to address ethical breaches ensure that everyone understands the importance of ethics and the consequences of ethical misconduct.

Seek Professional Development: Ethical leadership requires ongoing learning and growth. Leaders should proactively seek professional development opportunities to deepen their understanding of ethical principles, best practices, and emerging ethical issues in the nonprofit sector. Attending training programs, conferences, and workshops can enhance their ethical leadership skills.

Additionally, nonprofit leaders should regularly reflect on their own ethical decision-making processes, seek diverse perspectives when facing ethical dilemmas, and consult with stakeholders to ensure ethical considerations are taken into account in decision-making. By embracing ethical leadership practices, you set the foundation for an organization that operates with integrity, builds trust, and achieves its mission while making a positive impact on society.

Stakeholder Engagement and Inclusivity

To guarantee that different opinions are addressed and valued, nonprofit organizations should promote stakeholder involvement and inclusion. There are many approaches for increasing stakeholder participation and inclusivity.

Beneficiary Involvement: Nonprofits should actively include beneficiaries in decision-making processes. This entails soliciting their opinions, listening to them, and empowering them to participate in program development, implementation, and assessment. Nonprofits can better understand their beneficiaries' needs, interests, and goals by involving them in these processes, resulting in more successful and responsive programs. A health outreach nonprofit might invite local patients to co-design educational materials, ensuring that language and visuals reflect their cultural context.

Board Diversity and Inclusion: Nonprofit boards of directors should aim for diversity and inclusiveness. This includes ensuring diversity of backgrounds, such as gender, race, age, professional skills, and life experiences. Board diversity enriches conversations and decision-making processes by bringing multiple perspectives, ideas, and experience to the table, boosting the organization's capacity to manage complex issues and serve diverse communities.

Ethical Fundraising: To develop confidence with their contributors and stakeholders, nonprofits should follow ethical fundraising standards. This involves ensuring that all fundraising activities are transparent, honest, and accountable. Nonprofits should respect donor intent and privacy, eliminate conflicts of interest, and convey clearly how given funds will be utilized to achieve the organization's objective. Ethical fundraising strategies promote trust and confidence in the organization's operations and resource stewardship.

Fair Treatment of Employees and Volunteers: Nonprofits should treat its employees and volunteers with fairness, respect, and decency. This entails creating a safe and inclusive work atmosphere that embraces diversity and encourages equal opportunity. Nonprofits should assure equitable wages, give chances for professional growth and development, and acknowledge the efforts of its workers and volunteers. Creating a healthy and inclusive workplace culture develops a sense of belonging and inspires increased involvement and dedication.

Nonprofits may benefit from varied viewpoints, improve program efficacy, and develop strong connections with their beneficiaries, donors, workers, and volunteers by promoting stakeholder engagement and inclusion. These practices lead to a more egalitarian and inclusive nonprofit sector that actually fulfills the needs of the communities it seeks to influence.

Financial Stewardship and Accountability

Nonprofit organizations must practice prudent financial stewardship and accountability to guarantee resource effectiveness and stakeholder confidence. It is helpful to understand some fundamental strategies for financial stewardship and accountability.

Financial Transparency: Nonprofits should keep accurate and transparent financial records. This includes maintaining thorough and up-to-date accounting data, such as income and expense statements, balance sheets, and audits. They should give timely and accessible financial reports to stakeholders such as contributors, board members, and the general public. Adhering to accounting standards and complying with legal and regulatory regulations fosters transparency and provides stakeholders with a clear picture of the organization's financial health and how funds are used.

Resource Ethical Use: Nonprofits should use their resources efficiently, effectively, and in accordance with their goal. This entails using strong financial management methods, budgeting wisely, and monitoring expenditures to ensure that resources are directed toward attaining the desired results and maximizing impact. Avoiding wasteful activities like high overhead costs or unneeded spending indicates good resource stewardship.

Conflict of Interest: Nonprofits should develop rules and processes to identify, disclose, and manage conflicts of interest inside the organization. Conflicts of interest emerge when people's personal interests or ties have the potential to affect their decision-making or jeopardize the organization's best interests. Nonprofits may assure fairness, openness, and ethical decision-making by proactively resolving conflicts of interest. This might include requiring personnel to declare or disclose possible conflicts, recusing conflicted individuals from relevant decisions, or instituting review systems to assure neutrality. For instance, a board member who owns a catering company might recuse themselves from decisions about selecting food vendors for fundraising events

Whistleblower Protection: Nonprofits should put in place safeguards to protect whistleblowers who reveal unethical behavior or financial irregularities inside the organization. Whistleblower protection is developing a secure and private reporting procedure that encourages people to come forward with concerns or observations about wrongdoing. Protecting whistleblowers from retribution and taking proper action to address reported issues strengthens the organization's culture of accountability, openness, and integrity.

Nonprofit organizations that follow these principles demonstrate their commitment to prudent financial management and accountability. This not only helps to preserve stakeholder confidence, but it also ensures that resources are used properly and contribute to the organization's mission and community impact.

Data Privacy and Protection

Nonprofit organizations confront additional problems and obligations in preserving data privacy and guaranteeing the security of sensitive information in the digital era. Several issues are important to consider when dealing with institutional or stockholder data.

Data Governance: Nonprofits should develop explicit data governance rules and processes. Defining how data is gathered, kept, and utilized inside the company, as well as ensuring compliance with relevant data protection rules and regulations, are all part of this. Nonprofits may preserve openness, accountability, and legal compliance in their data management operations by implementing strong data governance procedures.

Informed Consent: Before collecting or utilizing personal information from individuals, nonprofits should get their informed consent. This includes properly describing the objective, extent, and potential hazards connected with data gathering and receiving individuals' explicit agreement. Giving people the ability to make informed decisions about how their data is used indicates respect for their privacy and autonomy.

Data Security: Nonprofits should put in place sufficient security measures to safeguard sensitive data from unauthorized access, loss, or misuse. This involves adopting encryption and safe storage mechanisms, routinely upgrading software and systems, and setting access restrictions to limit data exposure. Regular inspections and upgrades to security processes are required to handle emerging cybersecurity threats and vulnerabilities. A youth mentoring nonprofit might implement two-factor authentication and encrypted messaging to protect communications between mentors and participants.

Responsible Data Sharing: When sharing data with external partners or other parties, nonprofits should use prudence. They should verify that adequate data sharing agreements are in place before exchanging data to preserve the privacy and confidentiality of individuals' information. Nonprofits should carefully analyze external partners' data privacy and security procedures and only disclose data when necessary and with trustworthy entities.

Nonprofits should educate their employees and volunteers about data privacy and protection, foster a culture of data privacy awareness within the organization, and review and update their data privacy policies and practices on a regular basis to align with evolving regulations and best practices. These processes and safeguards secure the sensitive information nonprofits manage, preserve the confidence of their stakeholders, and keep their ethical responsibilities to respect individuals' privacy rights in the digital era by prioritizing data privacy and protection.

Ethical Decision-Making

Nonprofit organizations play a crucial role in addressing societal challenges and promoting positive change. To fulfill their missions effectively, it is essential for nonprofits to embrace ethical decision-making processes. Here are key practices for adopting ethical decision-making:

Stakeholder Consideration: Nonprofits should consider the interests and potential impacts of their decisions on all stakeholders. This includes beneficiaries, staff, donors, volunteers, and the wider community. By considering diverse perspectives and striving for fairness and equity, nonprofits can make decisions that prioritize social good and maximize positive outcomes.

Ethical Frameworks: Utilizing ethical frameworks or decision-making models can provide nonprofits with a structured approach to analyze complex ethical dilemmas. These frameworks help in evaluating different options, assessing potential consequences, and making ethically sound choices. They serve as guides to navigate difficult decisions and ensure alignment with ethical principles and values.

Confidentiality and Privacy: It is paramount to respect and uphold the confidentiality of sensitive information, especially when dealing with personal or sensitive issues. This involves seeking consent or legal authority before disclosing information and implementing robust confidentiality protocols to safeguard individuals' privacy rights.

Transparency and Accountability: Nonprofits should communicate decisions transparently to stakeholders, providing clear reasoning behind them. Transparency fosters trust and allows stakeholders to understand the organization's decision-making processes. Moreover, nonprofits should take responsibility for their decisions and be accountable for the outcomes, acknowledging any mistakes or shortcomings.

Continuous Learning and Improvement: Organizational leaders should engage in continuous learning and improvement by reflecting on ethical decisions and outcomes. By examining ethical challenges, nonprofits can identify opportunities for improvement and incorporate lessons learned into future decision-making processes. This commitment to learning and growth helps organizations adapt and enhance their ethical practices over time.

By embracing ethical decision-making processes, nonprofits demonstrate their commitment to ethical leadership, responsible governance, and the well-being of their stakeholders. Upholding high ethical standards not only strengthens the organization's reputation but also builds trust and credibility with donors, beneficiaries, and the community at large.

Ethical Considerations in Program Management and Evaluation

Ethical considerations are essential in program management and evaluation, guiding us to prioritize the well-being and rights of all involved. There are several considerations to note when implementing ethical review processes.

Equity and Inclusion: Promote equity and inclusion in program management and evaluation. Ensure that programs are accessible to all individuals, regardless of their socioeconomic status, background, abilities, or identities. Be mindful of potential biases and discrimination held by yourself and your personnel, striving to create a safe and inclusive environment for all participants.

Community Engagement: Engage with the community and stakeholders throughout the program management and evaluation processes. Ask for event feedback, foster meaningful partnerships, listen to diverse perspectives, and involve the community in decision-making. This collaborative approach ensures that programs address genuine needs and reflect the community's values and aspirations.

Ethical Data Handling: It is of paramount importance to adhere to ethical standards when collecting, analyzing, and reporting data. Obtain consent for data collection and use, ensuring anonymity and confidentiality. Take precautions to protect data from breaches or unauthorized access. Respect intellectual property rights and give appropriate credit to data sources and contributors.

Beneficiary Feedback: Create mechanisms for program participants and beneficiaries to provide feedback and voice their opinions. Actively seek their input on program design, implementation, and evaluation, but do allow options for anonymous feedback. Valuing their feedback empowers them as partners in the process and helps to improve program responsiveness and relevance.

Ethical Fundraising: Apply ethical principles to fundraising efforts. Ensure transparency in financial management, accurately represent the program's impact, and use funds responsibly and efficiently. Respect donor intent and provide regular updates on program outcomes to maintain trust and accountability.

Sustainability and Long-term Impact: Consider the long-term sustainability and impact of programs. Strive to create lasting change that benefits communities beyond the program's duration. Address environmental impacts, promote local capacity building, and foster community ownership of program initiatives. For example, a clean water project could teach local residents to maintain and repair filtration systems, ensuring the program's benefits continue after the initial funding ends.

Ethical Partnerships: Select partners and collaborators based on shared ethical values and principles. Conduct due diligence to ensure alignment with your organization's mission and ethical standards. Establish clear agreements that outline roles, responsibilities, and expectations to maintain ethical business partnerships.

Ethical Leadership: Foster ethical leadership within your organization. Set a tone at the top that emphasizes integrity, transparency, and ethical decision-making. Provide training and guidance to staff and volunteers on ethical practices, promoting a culture of ethics throughout the organization. Work to make sure your organizational leadership is guided by the mission.

Regular Ethical Reflection: Regularly reflect on ethical practices, dilemmas, and challenges faced in program management and evaluation. Foster a culture of continuous ethical reflection and improvement. Seek external guidance, such as ethical review boards or expert consultations, when dealing with complex ethical issues.

By incorporating these ideas to frame program ethics, your organization can uphold ethical standards, ensure the dignity of participants, and foster a positive and ethical program environment. Embracing ethical considerations demonstrates your commitment to responsible and impactful program management and evaluation.

CHAPTER 11:

ORGANIZATIONAL SUSTAINABILITY AND GROWTH

Introduction to Organizational Sustainability and Growth

Nonprofit organizations must be sustainable and expand in order to remain viable and have a long-term effect on their communities. In this chapter, we will look at tactics and factors that might help them develop long-term, sustainable organizations. Nonprofits may secure their capacity to execute their goals in an ever-changing context by concentrating on long-term viability, adaptation, and smart resource allocation.

More than simple financial stability is required for sustainability. Sustainability typically refers to the organization's ability to continue working, innovate, and adapt to new difficulties and opportunities. Building a sustainable and expanding organization involves careful planning, good leadership, and an organizational growth strategy.

Throughout this chapter, we will look at essential techniques and factors that can help nonprofit organizations achieve these goals. From expanding financing sources and building relationships to investing in people and fostering an innovative culture, each component is vital to the organization's long-term success.

Nonprofits may position themselves for long-term success and growth by implementing these tactics and taking into account the particular qualities of their organization and operational environment. As a result, they are able to optimize their influence, better serve their beneficiaries, and contribute to constructive social change.

Strategic Planning and Vision

Nonprofit organizations use strategic planning to define their future, generate development, and achieve long-term sustainability. We will look at essential factors that contribute to the creation of a successful strategic plan that will guide the organization's direction and actions.

Mission and Vision: A well-defined mission and vision statement serves as a compass for the business, offering a feeling of purpose and direction. The mission statement expresses the organization's primary purpose, whereas the vision statement describes the organization's intended future influence. When creating a strategic plan, it is critical to ensure that the mission and vision connect with the values and goals of the nonprofit.

Goals and Objectives: Strategic planning requires the establishment of specific, quantifiable goals and objectives. These objectives should be explicit, attainable, and aligned with the organization's mission and vision. Time-bound objectives should provide a path for the organization's growth and sustainability. Goals and objectives that are well-defined serve as progress markers and influence decision-making throughout the strategic planning process.

Environmental Scan: An environmental scan assists companies in understanding the internal and external elements that might affect their growth and sustainability. It entails studying larger socioeconomic, political, and technological trends as well as the organization's strengths, weaknesses, opportunities, and threats (SWOT analysis). Nonprofits may discover potential for development, foresee problems, and make educated strategic decisions by undertaking an environmental assessment. A food security nonprofit might identify an emerging need for mobile food distribution by noticing demographic shifts toward more elderly residents in its service area.

Stakeholder Engagement: Involving important stakeholders in the strategic planning process is critical for collecting varied viewpoints and establishing a complete strategy. Board members, workers, volunteers, beneficiaries, donors, and community members are examples of stakeholders. By integrating stakeholders, organizations can gain useful insights, enhance cooperation, and boost ownership and support for the strategic plan.

Action Plans: Creating action plans is a vital step in turning strategic goals into concrete activities. Action plans include the particular methods, actions, and resources needed to fulfill the organization's goals and objectives. Each action plan should clearly specify duties, dates, and performance metrics, guaranteeing accountability and supporting successful execution.

In addition to these features, it is critical to underline the need for frequent revision of the strategic plan. As the company matures and the external environment changes, periodic appraisal and revision of the plan is required to guarantee its relevance and effectiveness. Strategic planning evolves into a dynamic process that drives the organization's operations and allows it to adapt to changing demands and circumstances.

Resource Development and Fundraising

Effective resource development and fundraising strategies play a crucial role in sustaining and growing nonprofit organizations. Here, we can explore key approaches that can help nonprofits diversify their funding sources and maximize their financial sustainability.

Diversify Funding Sources: To minimize dependency on a single funding source, nonprofits should explore various avenues to generate revenue. This includes engaging in individual giving campaigns, seeking corporate partnerships and sponsorships, pursuing government grants, and exploring earned income opportunities. By diversifying funding sources, organizations can reduce vulnerability to fluctuations in funding and create a more stable financial base.

Donor Cultivation and Relationship Building: Building strong relationships with donors is essential for long-term sustainability. Nonprofits should implement donor cultivation strategies that focus on personalized communication, stewardship efforts, and recognition programs. By understanding donors' interests and motivations, nonprofits can better engage and cultivate their support, leading to increased loyalty and long-term commitment. For instance, a wildlife conservation group might invite major donors to participate in a guided release of rehabilitated animals, creating a memorable and personal connection to the mission.

Grant Writing and Management: Developing strong grant writing skills and effective grant management practices are vital for securing and managing grant funding. Nonprofits should invest in researching and identifying relevant grant opportunities, crafting compelling proposals, and ensuring efficient grant management and reporting processes. Building relationships with grant-making organizations and staying informed about their priorities and requirements can increase the chances of successful grant acquisition.

Social Enterprise: Exploring social enterprise opportunities can provide nonprofits with an alternative revenue stream while aligning with their mission. By developing revenue-generating ventures, such as the sale of merchandise, services, or innovative products, nonprofits can generate funds while also creating social impact. Social enterprises offer a sustainable and impactful way to generate resources beyond traditional fundraising methods.

Strategic Partnerships: Collaborating with other organizations, businesses, or government agencies can amplify the impact and financial sustainability of nonprofits. Strategic partnerships allow for resource-sharing, joint fundraising efforts, and the ability to reach a wider audience. By leveraging the strengths and expertise of partners, nonprofits can enhance their programs, increase their visibility, and secure additional funding opportunities.

In addition to these approaches, it is essential for nonprofits to continually assess and adapt their resource development and fundraising strategies based on changing trends, donor preferences, and the evolving needs of their beneficiaries. By implementing these strategies and being proactive in resource development, nonprofits can strengthen their financial sustainability and expand their capacity to create positive and lasting impact in their communities.

Organizational Capacity Building

Building organizational capacity is crucial for the long-term sustainability and growth of nonprofit organizations. By investing in this, nonprofits can improve their internal systems, better fulfill their mission, and adapt to the changing needs and challenges of their communities. There are a handful of key areas to focus on when it comes to exploring your capacity building.

Board Development: A strong and engaged board of directors is essential for effective governance. Ensure that your board members possess diverse expertise and networks that align with the organization's mission and strategic goals. Provide comprehensive board orientation, ongoing training, and opportunities for professional development. Engage board members in meaningful ways, leveraging their skills and connections to support fundraising efforts, strategic planning, and organizational oversight.

Leadership Development: Invest in developing the leadership capabilities of your staff members at all levels. Offer training programs, mentorship opportunities, and skill-building initiatives to enhance their management and leadership skills. By nurturing leadership talent within the organization, you can foster a culture of growth, innovation, and succession planning.

Human Resources Management: Establish effective human resources management practices to attract, retain, and develop talented individuals. Develop robust recruitment processes, implement performance management systems, and provide opportunities for staff development and training. Foster a positive and inclusive organizational culture that values diversity, collaboration, and employee well-being.

Technology and Infrastructure: Embrace appropriate technology systems and infrastructure to streamline operations and improve organizational efficiency. Invest in tools and software that support program management, data collection, analysis, and reporting. By leveraging technology effectively, nonprofits can enhance their capabilities in data-driven decision-making, communication, and resource management. An arts nonprofit could use an online ticketing and donor management platform to track attendance patterns, identify loyal patrons, and tailor future fundraising appeals.

Continuous Learning and Evaluation: Foster a culture of continuous learning and improvement within the organization. Encourage staff members to engage in professional development opportunities, stay informed about best practices in the sector, and actively participate in evaluation and reflection processes. Regularly assess program outcomes and impact, seeking opportunities to adapt and improve strategies based on lessons learned.

In addition to these areas, it is important for nonprofits to regularly assess their organizational capacity and identify areas for improvement. This can be done through self-assessments, external evaluations, and benchmarking against industry standards. By investing in capacity building, nonprofits can strengthen their internal systems, enhance their ability to achieve their mission, and effectively respond to the evolving needs and challenges of their communities.

Collaboration and Partnerships

Collaboration and partnerships are critical in ensuring nonprofit organizational sustainability and growth. Consider the below approaches in order to enhance community ties, program reach, and planning effectiveness.

Strategic relationships: Form strategic relationships with other nonprofits, corporations, government agencies, or community groups that have similar aims or serve comparable populations. Organizations can optimize their effect and achieve greater sustainability by working on joint projects or initiatives, pooling resources, and using collective experience.

Advocacy and Policy Engagement: Participate in advocacy activities to shape policies and systems that have a direct impact on the work of your organization and the communities you serve. You may magnify your voice and effect good change on a larger scale by collaborating with other groups and using collective lobbying efforts.

Collective Impact: Take part in efforts that bring together diverse stakeholders from many sectors to address difficult societal challenges. Organizations can work together to align their strategy, exchange resources, and coordinate actions in order to develop long-term, sustainable solutions that address core problems.

Knowledge Sharing: Share information, best practices, and lessons gained with other companies in the field. Participate actively in networks, conferences, and forums to exchange ideas, cooperate on initiatives, and remain current on emerging trends and possibilities. Nonprofits may jointly improve their objectives and impact by cultivating a culture of information sharing and cooperation.

Nonprofits must actively seek and cultivate practical collaborations. Organizations that collaborate can utilize their unique strengths, broaden their reach, and collaboratively address difficult social concerns. These relationships not only improve sustainability but also build a culture of innovation, learning, and shared achievement within the nonprofit sector.

Monitoring and Evaluation

Regular monitoring and evaluation are crucial components of nonprofit organizations' efforts to track progress, assess impact, and adapt strategies. Here are important practices to consider:

Performance Metrics: Develop key performance indicators (KPIs) that align with your organizational goals and objectives. These metrics should be measurable, relevant, and trackable over time. Regularly monitor and track these metrics to assess progress, identify areas for improvement, and make data-driven decisions that support sustainable organizational growth.

Impact Assessment: Conduct periodic impact assessments to measure the long-term effects and outcomes of your programs. Utilize evaluation methodologies and tools to assess the social, economic, and environmental impact created by your organization. Use the findings from these assessments to inform program adjustments, demonstrate impact to stakeholders, and communicate the value of your work.

Feedback Loops: Establish feedback loops to gather insights and perspectives from program participants, beneficiaries, and other stakeholders. Implement mechanisms such as surveys, interviews, focus groups, or suggestion boxes to actively collect feedback on program experiences, challenges, and suggestions for improvement. Incorporate this feedback into program design and delivery processes to ensure responsiveness to community needs. For example, a community health clinic might learn through patient surveys that evening hours are in high demand, prompting it to adjust operating times to better serve working families.

Learning and Adaptation: Foster a learning culture within the organization that encourages continuous improvement and adaptation. Create opportunities for staff members to reflect on successes and challenges, share lessons learned, and exchange best practices. Encourage the use of evaluation findings and feedback to inform decision-making and drive programmatic changes that lead to better outcomes.

By adopting these practices, nonprofit organizations can enhance their understanding of their work's impact, make informed decisions, and continuously improve their programs and services. Regular monitoring and evaluation help organizations stay accountable to their mission, optimize their resources, and maintain a focus on the community they serve.

CHAPTER 12

NONPROFIT SUSTAINABILITY IN CHALLENGING TIMES

Introduction to Nonprofit Sustainability in Challenging Times

Nonprofit organizations are not immune to difficulties and disruptions that might jeopardize their sustainability and capacity to achieve their purposes. Economic downturns, political instability, or public health emergencies can all have a substantial influence on the operations, funding, and general stability of charities. Nonprofits, on the other hand, may traverse these problems and assure long-term viability by proactively developing resilience and implementing successful solutions.

This chapter digs into considerations and techniques that nonprofit organizations may use to create resilience and sustain their influence in the face of adversity. It investigates financial management methodologies, fundraising diversification, strategic planning, risk assessment, and adaptive leadership. Nonprofits may fortify their organizations, weather uncertainty, and continue to make a positive influence in the communities they serve by understanding and applying these techniques.

Building resilience entails more than simply surviving difficult circumstances; it also entails thriving and adapting to change. Nonprofits that promote sustainability and resilience are better positioned to maintain services, engage stakeholders, and effectively adapt to their communities' changing needs. Nonprofits may overcome problems and emerge stronger in the face of adversity through careful planning, resource management, and a dedication to continual development.

Scenario Planning and Risk Management

In uncertain and challenging situations, nonprofit organizations can benefit greatly from scenario planning and risk management. These approaches help organizations anticipate potential disruptions, make informed decisions, and respond effectively to mitigate risks. By considering the following approaches, nonprofits can enhance their preparedness and navigate through uncertainties:

Scenario Planning: Nonprofits should engage in scenario planning to envision and prepare for potential challenges. This involves developing different scenarios that reflect a range of plausible future situations. By exploring these scenarios, organizations can identify potential risks, opportunities, and necessary adaptations. This proactive approach enables nonprofits to develop strategies that align with their mission and mitigate potential negative impacts. For example, a community arts nonprofit might prepare separate plans for a severe funding cut, an emergency shutdown, and a surge in public interest, so it can adapt quickly to each situation.

Risk Assessment: A comprehensive risk assessment is crucial for nonprofits to identify and understand the potential risks they face. By evaluating the likelihood and potential impact of each risk, organizations can prioritize their resources and develop appropriate risk mitigation strategies. This assessment should encompass various areas, including financial, operational, reputational, and programmatic risks. Regularly reviewing and updating the risk assessment allows organizations to stay responsive to emerging risks.

Contingency Planning: Nonprofits should develop contingency plans to outline specific actions to be taken in the event of various risks or crises. These plans should consider alternative funding sources, communication strategies, and program modifications to ensure continuity of operations. A food pantry could arrange agreements with multiple local suppliers so that if one source becomes unavailable, food deliveries to families are not interrupted. Contingency planning enables organizations to respond swiftly and effectively during challenging times, minimizing disruptions and maintaining their ability to deliver on their mission.

Financial Reserves: Building and maintaining financial reserves is crucial for nonprofit organizations to withstand unexpected financial challenges. By setting aside funds as reserves, nonprofits can create a buffer to help sustain their operations during periods of economic uncertainty or funding disruptions. Establishing clear policies and guidelines for reserve management ensures that these funds are used strategically and in alignment with the organization's long-term goals.

Incorporating scenario planning and risk management into the organizational culture allows nonprofits to be proactive, agile, and better equipped to navigate uncertainties. By anticipating and preparing for potential challenges, nonprofits can maintain their services, safeguard their stakeholders' interests, and continue making a positive impact even in the face of adversity.

Adaptability and Innovation

To thrive in challenging times, nonprofit organizations must prioritize adaptability and embrace innovation. By considering a variety of approaches, nonprofits can effectively navigate uncertainties and continue making a positive impact.

Agile Decision-Making: Nonprofits should cultivate a culture of agile decision-making, where staff members are empowered to make timely decisions and experiment with new approaches. This flexibility allows organizations to respond quickly to changing circumstances and adjust their strategies as needed. By encouraging staff to take calculated risks and learn from failures, nonprofits can foster a responsive and adaptable environment.

Flexibility in Program Delivery: Nonprofits should explore flexible program delivery models that can be adapted to accommodate changing circumstances. Leveraging technology and digital platforms can provide innovative ways to reach and engage beneficiaries, especially during challenging times. Embracing online tools, virtual platforms, and remote service delivery can enable nonprofits to overcome physical barriers and continue delivering their programs and services effectively. For example, A literacy nonprofit might switch from in-person tutoring to video conferencing sessions, mailing books and worksheets to participants' homes.

Collaboration and Partnerships: Nonprofits should actively seek strategic collaborations and partnerships with other organizations, businesses, and community groups. By pooling resources, knowledge, and expertise, nonprofits can enhance their sustainability and create a more significant impact. Collaborative efforts enable organizations to leverage complementary strengths, share costs, and collectively address complex challenges.

Innovation and Creativity: Nonprofits should foster a culture of innovation and creativity within the organization. Encouraging staff to think outside the box and explore new ideas allows nonprofits to find innovative solutions to emerging challenges. Creating an environment that embraces experimentation, learning, and continuous improvement can lead to the development of groundbreaking initiatives and approaches.

By prioritizing adaptability and innovation, nonprofits can stay ahead of the curve, remain relevant, and effectively serve their beneficiaries even in challenging times. Embracing change, seeking collaboration, and encouraging creativity positions them to navigate uncertainties with resilience and create lasting positive change.

Resource Diversification and Fundraising Strategies

During challenging times, nonprofit organizations must prioritize resource diversification and implement effective fundraising strategies to sustain their operations. Consider the following approaches:

Resource Diversification: Nonprofits should reduce their reliance on a single funding source by diversifying their revenue streams. This can be achieved by exploring opportunities for individual giving, corporate partnerships, earned income opportunities, and grants from diverse funders. By tapping into multiple funding channels, nonprofits can spread their financial risk and ensure a more stable resource base.

Donor Engagement and Stewardship: Building and maintaining strong relationships with donors is crucial. Nonprofits should actively engage donors through personalized communication, regular updates on program impact, and meaningful recognition of their contributions. By cultivating donor loyalty and trust, nonprofits can foster ongoing support and potentially attract new donors.

Crisis Fundraising: During challenging times, nonprofits can develop specific fundraising campaigns or appeals to address immediate needs or funding gaps arising from the crisis. It is important to clearly communicate the urgency and impact of the crisis to inspire donor generosity. Sharing compelling stories, leveraging social media platforms, and organizing virtual fundraising events can help mobilize support effectively. For instance, during a natural disaster, an animal rescue group could launch an emergency online fundraiser with live-streamed rescue updates to engage donors in real time.

Grant Monitoring and Reporting: Nonprofits should strengthen their grant monitoring and reporting processes to identify additional opportunities and ensure compliance with funder requirements. Timely and accurate reporting builds trust with funders and enhances the chances of receiving future funding. By effectively communicating the outcomes and impact of grant-funded programs, nonprofits can demonstrate accountability and the effective utilization of resources.

By diversifying resources and implementing effective fundraising strategies, nonprofits can better withstand challenging times and continue their vital work. Engaging donors, seeking new funding opportunities, and maintaining transparency in grant management contribute to the organization's sustainability and resilience.

Staff Support and Organizational Well-being

Supporting staff and prioritizing organizational well-being are crucial for nonprofit organizations to maintain sustainability during challenging times. Consider the following approaches:

Staff Well-Being: It is essential to prioritize the well-being of staff members by providing resources, support, and flexibility. This includes promoting work-life balance, offering mental health and wellness programs, creating a positive, inclusive work environment, and rewarding great work. By prioritizing staff well-being, organizations can foster a motivated and resilient workforce.

Professional Development: Investing in professional development opportunities for staff is vital to enhance their skills and adaptability. Offer training programs and workshops on topics such as crisis management, remote work strategies, and other relevant areas. This empowers staff to navigate challenges effectively and contribute to the organization's sustainability. An example of this would be a health services nonprofit training its staff in telehealth delivery methods to continue serving clients during extended clinic closures.

Transparent Communication: Maintain transparent and open communication with staff members during challenging times. Share regular updates about the organization's status, challenges, and successes. Involve staff in decision-making processes when appropriate, seeking their input and feedback. Transparent communication builds trust, fosters a sense of belonging, and encourages collaboration and resilience among staff.

Organizational Resilience: Build resilience within the organization by fostering a learning culture, promoting adaptability, and providing opportunities for innovation and growth. Encourage staff to embrace change, learn from challenges, and contribute ideas for improvement. By fostering a resilient organizational culture, nonprofits can navigate difficult times more effectively and sustain their operations.

By supporting staff and prioritizing organizational well-being, nonprofits can nurture a strong and dedicated workforce, enhance their adaptability, and maintain their sustainability even in challenging times.

Monitoring and Evaluation

Regular monitoring and assessment are critical activities for nonprofit organizations to assess the performance of their sustainability programs and make required improvements. This is particularly important in tumultuous business cycles.

Performance Metrics: It is critical to create and measure key performance indicators (KPIs) that match with the organization's sustainability goals. These metrics may include measures such as financial stability, program results, resource usage, and stakeholder satisfaction. Regular monitoring of these variables gives insights into progress and places for development.

Impact Assessment: Conducting periodic impact assessments helps firms to analyze the efficacy and long-term results of their sustainability strategy. This evaluation assists in determining whether the desired impact is being realized and gives insights into the organization's contribution to the community or cause it serves. It allows assessment of the efficacy of funding in situations when funding is more limited.

Learning and Adaptation: It is critical to cultivate a culture of learning and adaptation. It entails reflecting on both triumphs and problems, sharing lessons learned, and applying insights acquired to influence future decision-making. Organizations may enhance their sustainability efforts over time by continually learning and adjusting.

Stakeholder Feedback: Obtaining input from stakeholders such as recipients, donors, and partners is beneficial in understanding their views and requirements. This input may assist create sustainability initiatives and improve decision-making in order to better satisfy stakeholder expectations. Actively engaging stakeholders and adopting their feedback deepens the organization's connections and increases its influence.

Nonprofit organizations may measure the efficacy of their sustainability policies, find areas for improvement, and make informed decisions by applying these monitoring and evaluation methods. This cyclical process of learning and adaptation strengthens the organization's resilience and ability to successfully handle difficult times. Finally, it allows NGOs to continue accomplishing their purposes and making a good influence in the communities they serve.

CHAPTER 13:

SUSTAINING IMPACT AND EMBRACING CHANGE

Reflection on the Nonprofit Journey

As we near the end of this book, it's a good moment to pause and reflect on the incredible adventure you are taking. Creating and sustaining a nonprofit organization is a monumental task that demands devotion, endurance, and steadfast commitment. Before we say goodbye, let us take a minute to recognize your accomplishments and the great influence you can have on the world.

Consider the light that sparked your passion and prompted you to start down this path. Perhaps it was a passionate desire to solve a serious social issue, empower a marginalized group, or make a good difference in the lives of others. Whatever the impetus for your effort, it is critical to appreciate the courage and drive required to turn that first flicker into a reality.

Your journey undoubtedly had its share of difficulties and setbacks, and there will be more. You experienced obstacles that put your determination to the test as you followed your good objective. Funding limits, bureaucratic difficulties, and limited resources may have appeared to be significant obstacles at times. Nonetheless, you persisted (or you will persist) in exhibiting perseverance in the face of adversity.

Take pleasure in how you conquered these obstacles. Perhaps you used the potential of strategic alliances to multiply your influence by bringing together like-minded individuals and organizations. Perhaps you used creative techniques to create inventive answers, such as using technology or tapping into the expertise of your followers. You are successfully navigating the tumultuous seas by adapting, learning, and developing.

Now is the moment to recognize your accomplishments so far along this route. Remember the lives you've touched, the communities you've helped, and the change you aim to bring about. Each milestone is a step forward in your objective, a monument to your steadfast devotion and your team's hard efforts.

Hang onto the feeling of joy and thankfulness with us as we close this book. Recognize the significant influence you have had and will continue to have, not just on the people you have helped, but also on yourself. Treasure the connections you've built, the lessons you've learned, and the personal progress you've experienced.

May your path as a leader continue to inspire and elevate as you generate waves of good change in the globe. Congratulations on your accomplishments, and may your charitable organization prosper, making a lasting difference in the lives of people in need.

Embracing Change and Adaptation

Change is an inevitable component of the nonprofit sector's ever-changing landscape. To maintain your organization's long-term viability and performance, it is critical to view change as an opportunity for progress. You can adapt and grow in the face of changing problems by regularly reviewing the requirements of your beneficiaries and staying up to date on current trends and best practices.

One of the most important stages in embracing change is to keep an eye on the changing needs of your beneficiaries and the areas you serve. Engage with your stakeholders on a regular basis, asking their opinions and thoughts. Their insights are crucial in determining the effectiveness of your initiatives and finding areas for improvement. For example, a community food program might discover through feedback that families prefer fresh produce over packaged goods, prompting a shift in procurement priorities. You can guarantee that your business stays responsive and relevant by listening carefully and implementing their comments into your decision-making processes.

To successfully manage change, it is critical to keep current on emerging trends, research, and best practices in your sector. Create a learning culture in your firm by encouraging employees to pursue professional development opportunities and stay current on the newest innovations. Adopt an attitude of continual improvement, questioning the status quo, and experimenting with novel methods to addressing the complex societal concerns you want to solve.

Accepting change requires a willingness to explore, take measured risks, and innovate. Within your organization, foster a culture of creativity and inquiry in which new ideas are embraced and explored. Accept technology as a strong tool for increasing your impact, using its powers to reach a broader audience, streamline operations, and improve communication and fundraising efforts.

Furthermore, make diversity and inclusion essential principles in your organization. Recognize and respect the varied viewpoints, abilities, and experiences brought to the table by your team and stakeholders. By creating an inclusive workplace, you may tap into your team's combined expertise and creativity, allowing you to build more complete and successful solutions.

In addition, seek cooperation and partnerships to optimize your resources and widen your reach. Collaboration with other organizations, community stakeholders, and even for-profit corporations may result in synergies, shared knowledge, and a greater collective influence. By combining resources, skills, and networks, you may achieve considerably bigger results than would otherwise be feasible.

Accepting change and adapting to new situations is not always easy, but it is critical for the long-term success of your nonprofit organization. You can navigate the ever-changing terrain and continue to have a significant and sustained effect in the lives of people you serve by being open-minded, adaptable, and responsive. Accept change as a chance for progress, and allow it move you toward a future in which your company flourishes and continues to make a good effect in the world.

Nurturing Relationships and Building a Supportive Network

As it was when you began your nonprofit journey, it is still necessary to appreciate the importance of cultivating relationships and developing a supportive network. Your organization's success and survival are dependent not just on its programs and activities, but also on the quality of its relationships with funders, volunteers, staff, and partners.

Relationships with stakeholders are at the heart of your nonprofit's development and influence. Take the time to learn about their wants, worries, and dreams. Engage in open and meaningful interactions that allow you to listen carefully and learn from their viewpoints. By including people in creating your organization's future, you can guarantee that your efforts line with their expectations and make a genuine impact in their lives.

Invest in the growth of your staff to generate a strong network of support. Develop a culture of cooperation, respect, and constant learning inside your firm. Give your employees and volunteers opportunity for growth, training, and skill development. A youth services nonprofit might offer leadership workshops for volunteers interested in transitioning into more prominent program roles. Encourage them to take responsibility of their jobs and to contribute. Recognize and recognize their efforts, since their devotion and enthusiasm are vital assets in moving your cause forward.

Collaboration is essential for efficiently solving complex societal concerns. Create strategic alliances with other organizations, government agencies, and community groups that share same aims and values. You may increase your effect and generate long-term change by merging your resources, experience, and networks. Collaboration allows for the exchange of knowledge, the sharing of best practices, and the leveraging of collective capabilities, all of which result in higher achievements than any one business could achieve alone.

Remember that relationships or collaborations of any sort are not one-sided; they require continual maintenance and attention. Maintain constant contact with your funders, volunteers, staff, and partners. Keep them up to date on the development of your programs, the impact of their donations, and the difference they are making. Thank them for their help and acknowledge their participation in your organization's progress.

Building a supporting network entails more than just transactional encounters; it entails forging genuine ties based on shared values and a similar goal. You can inspire loyalty, dedication, and continuing involvement from your stakeholders by cultivating a feeling of belonging and community. Together, you can overcome obstacles, celebrate accomplishments, and navigate the nonprofit sector's ever-changing terrain.

As you move on, remember the power of connection and the strength of relationships. Nurturing these ties and creating a supporting network will not only improve the success and sustainability of your organization, but will also have a long-term influence on the lives of the individuals you serve.

Staying Resilient in the Face of Challenges

As a charity leader, you will undoubtedly face obstacles and failures along the way. Numerous external variables, like financial uncertainty, political upheavals, and unanticipated catastrophes, have an impact on the nonprofit sector. However, it is at these trying moments that your strength and dedication to your cause truly show.

To handle the challenges that come your way, it's critical to keep focused on your organization's purpose and have a clear understanding of the effect you want to create. Ground yourself in your goals and allow them to drive your decisions and actions. This sense of purpose will drive your determination and motivate your team to overcome difficulties and develop inventive solutions.

Building organizational resilience is essential for dealing with uncertainty. Establishing cash reserves and diversifying your financing sources might act as a financial cushion during times of financial stress. Investigate ways to involve individual contributors, business partners, and grantmakers in order to lessen dependency on a single funding source. This multifaceted strategy will assist you in maintaining stability and adapting to changes in the financial landscape.

Another important part of resilience is the creation of contingency plans. Anticipate foreseeable problems and devise solutions to them. Establish procedures, communication channels, and reaction systems to prepare for unanticipated disasters. With a well-thought-out strategy in place, you can respond to crises quickly and efficiently, reducing their impact on your organization and the people you serve. For instance, a coastal conservation group might have evacuation and relocation protocols for staff and equipment in case of hurricanes.

Remember that you are not alone in dealing with these difficulties. Seek assistance from your network of nonprofit leaders, mentors, and support groups. Participate in information exchange, problem-solving collaboration, and peer learning. You can get useful insights and views that will help you manage challenging situations by harnessing the collective expertise and experiences of others.

Take use of the resources that are available to you. Investigate and connect with local and national support groups that offer nonprofit-specific information, training, and help. These resources can provide knowledge, financial possibilities, and networks to help your organization thrive and flourish.

Staying resilient in times of uncertainty necessitates adaptation and the capacity to embrace change. Maintain an open mind to new ideas, novel techniques, and developing trends in your profession. Assess your strategy, plans, and operations on a regular basis to guarantee they stay relevant and successful. Adopt a culture of learning and improvement in which feedback is appreciated and lessons learnt are used to better your methods.

While obstacles can put your resilience to the test, they also provide possibilities for development, creativity, and significant change. You can handle uncertainty with purpose and continue to have a meaningful effect on the communities you serve by staying focused on your mission, creating organizational resilience, seeking help, and being adaptive.

Celebrating Milestones and Recognizing Achievements

As you traverse the rewarding yet challenging route of heading a nonprofit organization, it is critical to celebrate the milestones and recognize the accomplishments that have molded your journey. Each step forward takes you closer to accomplishing your vision and creating a lasting difference in the lives of the people and places you serve.

As you celebrate your accomplishments, remember to thank your employees, volunteers, and supporters for their devotion and hard work in propelling your organization's success. Recognize their efforts and thank them for their dedication to your objective. Their enthusiasm and steadfast support have acted as catalysts for good transformation.

Sharing success stories is an effective method to engage your stakeholders and celebrate your team's achievements. Highlight your organization's transformative influence on individuals and communities. Use narrative to convey real-life experiences, testimonies, and testimonials that demonstrate the impact you have made. This could include sharing the story of a single mother who secured stable housing through the organization's assistance, showing the tangible results of donor support. This not only recognizes accomplishment but also builds pride and connection among your followers.

Remember to celebrate not just large achievements, but also small victories along the road. These small victories are the building blocks of advancement that demonstrate the good progress you are making. You can excite your team, increase morale, and maintain a sense of momentum and purpose by recognizing and celebrating these events.

It is also critical to reflect on the lessons acquired both from your successes and disappointments. They are both precious chances for development and advancement. Analyze the successful strategies and those that may be improved and use the insights you gain to improve your techniques, increase your impact, and continue to grow and progress as a company.

As you begin on the next stage of your charity adventure, remember to take regular breaks to reflect on longer-term accomplishments. Take time to enjoy those accomplishments, thank those who have helped, and accept the lessons they taught. You will energize the spirit of your company, encourage sustained devotion, and move your purpose forward with newfound vigor and enthusiasm by doing so.

CONCLUSION:
A NEVER-ENDING JOURNEY

Starting and running a nonprofit organization is a unique and rewarding enterprise that demands devotion, tenacity, and a strong desire to make a positive impact in the world. It is critical to remember that you are not alone on this path. As you continue, it is critical to adopt a mentality of continual learning, adaptability, and development. Keep up with the latest trends, research, and best practices in your profession. Being open to change and innovation, as well as understanding new ways and ideas, may better serve your objective and lead to a more substantial effect.

Maintain a strong connection to your organization's mission and the communities you serve. Regularly review the changing needs and goals of individuals you seek to assist, and ensure that your programs and initiatives stay relevant, impactful, and responsive to their changing circumstances. Remember that collaboration and partnerships are essential instruments for increasing your influence. Build ties with other nonprofits, government agencies, community groups, and others who have similar interests. By joining forces, you may better harness group skills, resources, and experience to address difficult societal concerns.

As you travel through this adventure, be prepared to take calculated chances and step outside of your comfort zone. Innovation and experimentation may result in game-changing breakthroughs and dramatic organizational shifts. Embrace innovative technology and digital platforms to broaden your reach, improve productivity, and engage a larger audience.

Above all, remember the difference you're making in the world. Celebrate the small and large accomplishments along the journey. Recognize and thank your teams, volunteers, and supporters for their contributions to bringing your purpose to reality. You can create an environment that encourages and inspires everyone involved by cultivating a culture of appreciation and celebration.

The nonprofit sector needs enthusiastic and visionary leaders like you as you begin each new chapter of your career. Your dedication to effecting change is critical. Stay focused on your mission, be resilient in the face of adversity, and never lose trust in the transformational potential of your work. Thank you for beginning this great adventure and for your unshakable commitment to making the world a better place. May your journey be filled with purpose, resilience, and continuous success as you make a lasting difference in the lives of those you serve.

Together, we can create a better future for everybody.